In the 1950s many people made the great leap into the unknown and migrated to Canada. In the hope of a better life, a young Scotswoman and her family found themselves on a remote farm in the Prairie lands of Alberta.

In a superbly written account of their adventures, Margaret Gillies Brown tells the story of the highs and lows of settling in the New World and of the realities of a great migration.

Far from the Rowan Tree is a moving, evocative and ultimately affirming story of human energy and initiative.

previous books by the same author:

Give me the Hill-run Boys (Outposts Pub.)
Voice in the Marshes (Outposts Pub.)
Hares on the Horizon (Outposts Pub.)
No Promises (Akros)
Looking Towards Light (Blind Serpent Press)
Footsteps of the Goddess (Akros)

Far from
the Rowan Tree

Margaret Gillies Brown

Argyll
publishing

© Margaret Gillies Brown

First published 1997
This edition 1998
Argyll Publishing
Glendaruel
Argyll PA22 3AE
Scotland

Subsidised by the Scottish Arts Council

**British Library Cataloguing-in-Publication Data.
A catalogue record for this book is available from
the British Library.**

ISBN 1 874640 69 6

Cover design Creative Link, North Berwick

Cover Photo Courtesy Canadian Tourism Commission

Origination Cordfall Ltd, Glasgow

Printing Colourbooks Ltd, Dublin

Oh! Rowan Tree, Oh! Rowan Tree
Thou'lt aye be dear to me
Intwin'd thou art
Wi mony ties o hame and infancy

Scots song
by Carolina Lady Nairne

Emigrant Journey

There was the journey,
The endless coming on of the same wave,
The no-land time of ocean and high hopes
Until the icebergs rose
Like white snow palaces . . .
There were the moving days
And weary nights of train-hours overland,
The trees, the lakes, the straight and rolling plains
Until time stopped in sheer fantasy
Of a pre-dawn winter morning –
Gloved hand swinging the iron-hard handle
Of a frozen water pump
At the edge of a bark-rough cabin;
Above, the sky, moving strange magnificence,
Voile curtains of colour
Changing, shifting imperceptibly;
Below, the star-sparkled snow –
A virgin's looking glass
Where spruce trees shot the only shadows
That made no movement –
Silence, immensity of silence,
Oil fires were burning brands
Reaching for chiffon robes
Of an aurora of dancers
Repeating dream sequences . . .
I tried to wake from unreality,
Felt my spine freeze,
Heard coyotes howling down the night.

Foreword

After the second World War and in the 1950s in particular, a great many people left the shores of Britain for other countries. They were much encouraged to do so especially by the governments of both Canada and Australia who were seeking to fill up their vast empty lands with people from the west.

Every newspaper carried glowing advertisements hoping to entice people to take the leap into the unknown. Most towns had recruiting offices to cope with enquiries by those wanting to leave for 'lands of opportunity'. Britain was in the doldrums in the aftermath of war and the progress of recuperation was slow. The Scots, always a people of emigration and adventuring, were not behind in this exodus.

In the vanguard went one young Scottish couple with three pre-school age children choosing to go to Alberta, an as yet little-known state in western Canada, reputed to be emerging as an oil-rich province – a frontier land at the hindmost area of the prairies where the great Rocky Mountains rose as a bastion before the Pacific Ocean.

Canada held out attractive lures of assisted passages and worthwhile jobs in the western provinces – from the gold mines at Yellow Knife in the North West Territories to the farming of almost virgin soil in Alberta.

This particular family elected to pay their own passage but to go under the auspices of the Canadian National Railway. It would be a long journey – five days by ship over the Atlantic and four days on the Transcontinental train, *The Prairie Schooner*, crossing a vast sea of land in the white grip of an Arctic winter, to Edmonton. There they were to be allocated a job on a farm and a furnished house, somewhere in Alberta. Little did they know what lay in store for them.

Margaret Gillies Brown
Errol, Scotland February 1997

Contents

Redwoods, Red Deer, Alberta
St Valentine's Day 1959

At 4am on that first February morning after we arrived at Redwoods, I stepped outside our shack standing all on its own in the very heart of the Westlands. Many coloured curtains of light shifted across the dark bowl of night. Their silent, wide sweeping movements, reminded me of searchlights in wartime. But they had been dull in comparison to these shot silk waves of brilliance. Moving, with a sense of excitement, these Northern Lights, these Merry Dancers, swayed backward and forward and were reflected on a field of virgin snow that stretched on and on beyond the sight of human eye. At intervals, from the rainbow-coloured earth, great orange flames leaped upward like wild demons. Oil had been found here; these flames were manifestations of the burning off of natural gas that would otherwise have exploded underground or spread poisonous fumes into the atmosphere.

The scattered clumps of dark spruce trees alone were still. I stood in amazement – just looking. Never in my wildest dreams had I imagined or expected such spectacular beauty.

I didn't stand for long. It was intensely cold. With gloved hand I took hold of the freezing cast-iron handle of the pump that stood at the side of the shack. With vigorous movements I jerked it up and down. It was quite some time before water appeared and when it did it gushed out in great spurts, spilling over the battered kettle's rim and freezing instantly on my shoes.

Then I heard them! They broke the silence like

banshees, frightening the night. My heart froze within me. What beasts made so eerie a sound? – Were they hungry? – Had they smelled human flesh. I hurried back into the shack and quickly closed the rickety door.

It was warm inside. Life came back into my heart and limbs. I could feel my cheeks glowing. The oil heater in the corner of the boys' bedroom gave off a steady glow. Heat came also from the cast-iron cook-stove which I had banked up with green logs before going to bed. It wasn't quite out. I poked it. It spluttered into life. Slowly flames began to curl round the fresh logs. I placed the kettle on the fire. It was a very old one and had a small leak in the bottom which caused the hotplate to hiss and spit at regular intervals. I heard movement coming from the couch behind me and a voice thick with sleep saying, "My God! where am I . . . ?"

Chapter I

Westward Look the Land is Bright
(4th February 1959)

I woke to find a bright ray of winter sun had drifted up the eiderdown that covered the large hotel bed and had landed on my white pillow. It was a moment or two before dream gave way to reality. This was the day I had been waiting for – the beginning of the long journey – the start of an adventure. I looked at my watch; eight thirty. Time enough.

I lay back on the pillow, enjoying the crisp feel of the linen sheets and snuggled into my sleeping companion. How young he looked I thought; how untroubled after all he'd been through. It's a wonder it didn't show more. Six years ago we'd met and fallen in love. Six months later we were married. He hadn't changed much. For a moment I studied the fine features which had first attracted me – the high forehead, the slightly receding chin, less noticeable now because of the moustache he had grown. His face, more weathered than it used to be, was still tanned even after the long cold winter we had had. His face and limbs had been bronzed when we first met.

"Permanent," he told me laughingly, one day when we were still courting. "All sailors have tans."

He had been through five years of war before I met him, joining the Royal Navy as soon as he was old enough. His hair at the front drew back from a widow's peak. He'd worried about this when he was younger, imagining he was going bald. Now I stroked it with my finger and he woke, blinked and asked the time in the thick voice of sleep.

I slid my awkward body out of the big bed. My feet touched the soft hotel carpet. It was a glorious morning. The sun, climbing above the hills on the other side of the River Tay, threw brilliant diamonds of light into the water.

During the night snow had fallen on Dundee – just enough to dust the roof tops that now, caught by the early rays, glowed in palest crimson. Spirals of smoke from morning chimneys went straight upwards. The road running in front of the hotel was busy – buses, cars, bicycles, people on the pavements, all hurrying to work. Not so long ago trams had rattled and swayed along this way. Things were changing in Scotland, but slowly.

Suddenly the bedroom door burst open and our three young sons tumbled into the room.

"When do we go Mum?"

"As soon as we've dressed, packed our night things and had breakfast."

The smell of bacon wafted upstairs. In half an hour we were in the dining room all packed and ready to go. The two oldest boys had dressed themselves today without the usual fuss or argument and they had helped to dress wee Ronnie. We ate well – our last Scottish breakfast for the foreseeable future: porridge, bacon and egg, toast and marmalade, tea.

My mother and father were at the station to see us off. My vivacious mother, dressed brightly as always in a red coat and white scarf, looked cheerful this morning, no trace of tears. Tears were for yesterday.

How old was she, I momentarily wondered? She never would tell us. Her black hair refused to go grey, only strands here and there which, from time to time, she painted in the privacy of her room. Her cheeks were pink with rouge and her lips bright with lipstick which she hadn't applied quite carefully enough. Dad stood beside her, tall, more serious and dressed as always in sober browns. Until last night we had lived with them for three months following the sale of our sheep farm. They had been most helpful to us but I knew they must be tired.

This bright morning, even Dundee's large, draughty, smoke-grimed station looked fresh. There was a general air of energy about – people coming and going all the time. The sun penetrated the high panes of glass held in place by Victorian fretwork. Waiting engines threw up clouds of steam. The boys were excited at the sight of long trains, black stokers and red fire and by the noise – the clatter and clank of wheels. We had to watch they didn't go too near the edge and the big drop down onto the track.

Ronald soon had all our overnight luggage aboard. The rest had gone on ahead to Liverpool all marked in large red letters: GILLIES, EDMONTON STATION, ALBERTA, CANADA. Richard and Michael, the oldest boys, four and three, climbed into the train unaided. I followed and Ronald, with wee red-haired Ronnie, eighteen months old, held in his arms, brought up the rear. The seats of the carriage were straight-backed. Black and white pictures of idyllic holiday spots in Britain looked down at us from the walls while steam blew up from underneath the train and the carriage smelt faintly of tar.

Ronald's father hadn't come to see us off. He didn't like station farewells and he hadn't wanted us to go to Canada anyway.

"Remember to write as soon as you can and be careful." I registered the note of anxiety in mother's voice. "When you get settled go and see a doctor and make sure that everything's all right."

I assured her I would. The train began to move. The children and I blew our last kisses. Ronald waved. Their figures grew smaller and smaller until, rounding a corner, we lost sight of them altogether – our journey had begun.

We were fortunate to have a carriage to ourselves.

"When will we see them again?" asked Richard, his blue eyes larger than usual. His words broke into my thoughts – a paradox – the sadness of parting yet how good it was to get away at last to our chosen but unknown destination.

"When we get settled and have been at our new home for a while they will fly over to see us. It's not like the old days when grown up kids went from home to far away places. For them it might be many years before they saw their mums and dads again – if ever."

"What sort of house will we be living in?"

Ronald answered this time. "We don't know yet. We'll just have to wait and see but it won't be like our old stone-built farmhouse. It might be made of wood. It might be a log cabin

15

like you see in some of your picture books, but more likely it will look like this one. With that Ronald took out from the inner pocket of his warm camel hair coat an envelope and pen and drew a simple villa.

"Remember the day mum and I went to Glasgow to see the man about going to Canada? Well he showed us a book about different farms in Saskatchewan and this is how most of the pictures of houses on the farms looked."

"But I thought we were going to Alberta."

"Yes, so we are but I expect houses will be similar there. Alberta hasn't been so long settled. They didn't actually have pictures of Albertan farms to show us."

"Will we be living amongst hills like we did at home?"

"It's possible – we could be in the foothills of the Rockies but we won't know where we are going till we get to Edmonton. A man at the station will tell us where to go from there."

"Will there be sheep and cows on the farm like the ones we had?"

"I don't know, Richard."

I detected a note of impatience in Ronald's voice at all those questions he wasn't able to answer. But distraction came as the train slowed and, with a squeal of brakes, came to a rather abrupt halt at a small station. Wee Ronnie tumbled off the seat making a noise louder than any squealing brakes – Gleneagles. The other two looked out the window while I rescued Ronnie screaming from the floor. Two passengers got into a first class carriage near the engine. A man in a tweed coat and hat and an elegant woman in a fur coat.

The train did not stop long and once more we were rattling through the sunny countryside. Richard and Michael were on their knees on the carriage seats with noses glued to the window as bridges and houses, cattle and sheep, the whole diversity of the Scottish landscape flew past. When they got tired of looking they began to play with the toy cars their grandad had given them before they left, each one a different colour. Michael, looking his usual angelic self with his brown curls and slightly hooded eyes, switched cars when Ronnie wasn't looking. Red-haired, bullet-headed Ronnie went into an instant fury.

"How like your father he is," I said to Ronald. "Impatient – ready to flare up at anything, determined to get his own way."

"Yes," said Ronald laughing. "Once in a lifetime is enough. One of the reasons I'm leaving Scotland – is to get away from the old man." His actions however belied his words as he picked up his youngest son affectionately and tried to calm him.

Ronald and his father had never got on well together. Ronald was not the sort of son his father had wanted, not robust, not football-playing, not the cold-showers-in-the-morning hard physical worker. Lindsay, his father, had never understood his son's love of art and books and, when he grew older, never approved of his party-going. Ronald was brilliant at a party – a natural comedian he could make everyone laugh. As a teenager I had been dreamy and over-serious. I never really knew what fun was till I met Ronald.

That was a night to remember – the night we first met at the nurse's annual dance held in the Empress Ballroom down by the Dundee docks. Not that his father was a bad sort. He had been good to us at the Shanry Farm. But how Ronald had hated his unexpected visits early in the morning to see if he was up – and he wasn't always up – not if there had been a party the night before. I had to say he was out on the hill.

It was dark by the time we reached Liverpool

"There is no sensation quite like a ship departing – nothing quite so heart-rending as a ship slowly leaving its moorings. The people on the shore all waving and the people on the ship all waving and the distance between getting ever greater."

Ronald had often told me this before we decided to emigrate. That was why he didn't want my people or his people to see us off. He knew! Serving in the Navy during the war he had many departures.

For me, leaving my homeland was a new experience. I had always wanted to travel but on the pay of a nurse in training in the early fifties it was impossible. Hostelling, on a bicycle round the Highlands, was as much as I could afford.

Next morning we left the rundown hotel, where we had stayed the night, by taxi. At Liverpool docks the *Sylvania* lay waiting, her white bulwarks gleaming in the weak winter sunlight.

Richard and Michael were especially excited, bouncing up the gang plank a bit ahead. Ronald followed them smartly, carrying wee Ronnie and I brought up the rear. Ronald had been worrying about boarding the ship with all our luggage and the children. His worries had been unnecessary. Everything was well-organised and had gone smoothly. He had also worried about our accommodation – offered to pay more for a cabin above the Plimsoll line where we could all be together. We were told this wasn't possible unless we went first class. Again we needn't have worried. We got one of the best cabins in the tourist class. It had four bunks, four large cupboards, a cot in the middle, a lavatory, washhand basin and shower. Strips of polished pine lined the walls. The children tried all the bunks, turned on all the taps, pulled the lavatory chain and gazed out of the porthole fascinated to see the sea so near to them.

As *Sylvania* pulled away from the wharfside we went up on deck to have a last look at our homeland. I watched the frantically waved handkerchiefs, the blown kisses, the tears of farewell. I was glad there was no one to see us off. For a while we watched as the gap widened between ship and shore but the children were eager to get back to the cabin and explore the ship further. I was glad of the distraction.

Chapter 2

The Clear Cold Air of Halifax

Five days later we disembarked into a freezing Halifax. The air was more bitingly cold than anything we had felt before. The sky was a vivid steel blue. On the street, by the wharfside of this Nova Scotian town, snow had been packed hard by passing vehicles. Some of it had been swept off, presumably just after it had fallen, and lay in grubby thick furrows lining the road. The few men out and about wore quilted parkas with fur-lined hoods. They spoke a pleasant but different English. We were in a different land.

It was early in February – the middle of a Canadian winter – a long time yet till we could hope for warmer weather. The man in the Glasgow emigration office hadn't wanted us to come so soon.

"April would be a better month," he had advised. "Nothing much happens on the land till April."

But we were anxious to get away. The farm would be sold at the November term and after that we would be living with my family which, with the best will in the world, would become difficult for all of us after a time.

"Well," said the emigration man, "if you're determined to go in winter, the first ship of the season sails on the first week of February. I'll book you in on that. You will have to disembark at Halifax. It's too soon to get up the St Lawrence. It will still be frozen over. It's a long journey by train to Alberta."

I walked down the gang plank of the *Sylvania* without regret that the sea voyage was over. Latterly I had enjoyed the camaraderie of other emigrants and the fun but had never felt really well. Already with ground solid under my feet and in sharp bright air, I felt better. A thrill of joy, as enervating as the frost, as

bright as the sun, went through me. At last the promised land –
a land of ice and fire, someone had called it, a land I had always
wanted to see as far back as I could remember. Perhaps, ever
since the first time I become aware of Pink Foot and Grey Lag
geese, in great skeins, flying from the reedbeds edging the river
below our hillside home. Mother had told me these birds flew
all the way from the frozen wastes of Canada where they nested
to be with us in winter. She was wrong about the country but it
didn't matter. She was an incurable romantic and had the power
to invest with a sort of magic any tale she told my sister and me.
And, as soon as I was able to read long books, she gave me one
called *Out of the Westland,* a story set in Canada earlier in the
century. I had been entirely captivated by this book. Part of the
story took place in Edmonton, our destination. Reading it, at a
later date, I found it geographically totally inaccurate (the author
had placed Edmonton in the Arctic circle for instance) but just
the same I think he must have been to Canada as he had
captured the essence of it. On the wharfside in Halifax it was
already living up to this essence.

Ronald took my hand in case I should slip on the snow. The
children danced around us. We were directed towards a huge
barren warehouse of a building where we were met at the doors
by uniformed officials who began herding us, rather like cattle
at the market, into two separate parts – the men into one end of
the building partitioned off as a customs house, and women
and children into the other. Ronald was none to pleased at being
separated from us so abruptly. He was even less pleased at the
amount of time he had to wait in the custom house. He told me
all about it later on in the day.

It seemed to take a long time before the immigrant's luggage
began to trickle through from the *Sylvania* and longer still till
ours appeared. Ronald thought it was never going to come. There
were two men officiating and a woman. They were all in uniform
but the men wore open-neck shirts. Ronald had plenty of time
to observe them. The men looked OK, Ronald reckoned, but
the woman looked hard-faced, grim-mouthed and mean. He
hoped he wouldn't get her. He watched as they dealt with the
luggage of our shipmates. Some of them were let through without

anything being opened up; some had their luggage casually looked through without much disturbance of goods. He could see signs of anger on some of the faces of those who had been unfortunate enough to get the woman although he didn't catch what it was she said that made them angry. Eventually Ronald's turn and it was that awful woman.

"Open up," she said with no preliminaries.

Our cases and trunks had been securely fastened and it took some time to undo all the straps and locks.

"Hurry up – haven't got all day!" said the woman.

Do you want me to open them all?"

"Yes all!" she snapped. "Don't know what you effete English might have in there."

Ronald had said nothing up to this point, knew better than to argue with her but now really incensed he said,

"I'm not English." Not that Ronald had anything against the English. He had many English friends. It was the way she said it that annoyed.

"Oh well, Scots, Irish – it's sure all the same. You're in Canada now."

Ronald kept silent while she removed everything from our carefully packed cases and trunks. She made sarcastic remarks, here and there, while doing so.

"These fancy shirts – what do you think you're going to do with them? You're going to Alberta I see. What are you going to do there?"

"Farming," Ronald replied, "although it's really none of your business."

"Oh dirt farming," she replied. "You sure have the wrong clothes for that."

At last she had come to the bottom of the last trunk where our evening clothes lay carefully wrapped in tissue paper. She took them out of their wrappings, my lacy sky blue dance dress, Ronald's evening suit. Holding our clothes at arm's length she gave a sarcastic laugh

"Look at these, you guys!" she said to the other officials who were standing idly by, all the other immigrants having gone. "And he says he's going dirt farming in Alberta."

21

"He sure won't need them there," one of the men said.

Ronald suppressed his anger with difficulty as he put everything back into cases and trunks. It took some time.

The children and I fared better. We were shown to hard wooden benches along with the other women and children from the ship and told to sit there till our husbands returned. I wondered how long we would have to wait. All of us were clad in winter coats and were beginning to feel the heat. The high wooden warehouse was surprisingly warm.

Besides those of us who had disembarked from the *Sylvania*, there were a number of Canadian women in the building, They wore no coats and were mostly middle-aged to elderly. Some wore unremarkable skirts and jerseys. Others wore jeans and trousers even although their figures were sometimes far from elegant. This was a surprising sight for us coming from douce Scotland where, in those days, few women wore trousers and especially not older women. Some women were in uniform, the most recognizable being the maroon and navy garb of the Salvation Army with its long coat and old fashioned bonnet. All these women from church and charity began to bear down on us – especially those of us with children.

"Welcome to Canada. We sure hope you like it here. Is there anything we can help you with. How about the children – anything you need?"

As they moved on, going from one to the other they each gave us something for the children – a small toy, book, miniature packet of cereal. The boys were captivated by the bright white, red and blue individual packets with their tantalizing pictures of crunchy flakes being poured into a plate, something they hadn't seen before in austere Scotland. Michael started to open his packet of flakes.

"No Michael, not just now," my voice was firm and I managed to persuade him otherwise.

"Look," I said pointing to the picture on the packet. "You're meant to put them in a plate and eat them with milk and sugar just like cornflakes at home. They're much better that way. Wait till we get on the train." And I stowed them away among the hand luggage. To distract the boys from the gaudy packets I opened up one of the books they had been given. A story in bright pictures of animals, gophers and coyotes, neither of which they had ever heard of before. I told them they would probably see them in the fields round their new home.

It was a couple of hours or more before Ronald returned. I noticed his angry expression as soon as he entered.

"Damned woman!" he exploded. "What a nasty piece of work she was! Most people took about ten minutes to get through customs once they got their luggage but she had to go through everything of ours. I think she took delight in knocking me."

"I wondered where you'd got to. I was watching for you, saw the others come through. Never mind, you're here now, that's the main thing, and we've been well looked after."

Ronald suddenly noticed all the extra things I had accumulated while he was away.

"Where on earth did all this come from?" he said.

"A host of do-good ladies." I replied, "from various churches and institutions."

Ronald glowered but said nothing. I knew what he was thinking. All this charity was hurtful to his pride and I didn't realize, until later, how bruised it had been by the customs woman or how she had shaken his confidence.

"Where do we go from here?"
"To the railroad station," he said.
I noticed he had already changed the terminology.

"It was very kind of them," I said. "They welcomed us to Canada and asked if there was any way they could help us. I couldn't think of anything at the time but I can now," I laughed. "We need help to transport all this extra baggage."

Ronald said nothing and I quickly changed the subject.

"What now?" I asked, "where do we go from here?"

"To the railroad station," he said. I noticed he had already changed the terminology.

The station buildings were bright and airy, modern and warm

to the point of being stuffy, another new experience for us after the draughty Scottish stations to which we were accustomed. On entering we all got a surprise when the high glass doors magically opened in front of us. The train for Montreal was due to leave in the evening. It was now about lunch time. Ronald and I debated whether we should explore Halifax but decided it was too difficult an operation with the children and luggage. Also, by this time, I had a sore throat and it was severely cold out there. We lunched on sandwiches, coffee and juice from the cafeteria. The enormous sandwiches bore little resemblance to those back home. Huge by comparison, they were filled with crisp lettuce, juicy tomatoes, the tastiest of cheese.

The afternoon passed pleasantly enough. There were other children for ours to play with and the toys they had all been given kept them happy for hours. Most of the passengers that had been on board the *Sylvania* were waiting for the same train as we were, so we had no lack of company.

Eventually a loudspeaker announcement told us that our train was ready to board. Again those magic doors opened without us having to lay a finger on them. The boys were mystified and wanted to go back into the waiting area to have it happen again. After the warmth of the waiting room the cold air hit us all the more severely. Once through the doors we found ourselves surprisingly close to the snow-encrusted rails on which the train hissed patiently. We could have touched them – there was no raised platform as at home. I looked up, up, up at the train. It seemed at least twice as tall as any of the trains back home. It made me feel small and for the first time it got through to me that my usual scale of size must change. In this huge country perhaps everything was bigger. I looked along the length of the train. It disappeared into the blackness, seeming to go on forever. Its brass bell swayed and clanged loudly in temperatures well below zero – the sound had a impersonal, hollow ring to it. For once the boys were overawed. Ronald lifted them up on to the iron steps and into the train without a word being said.

Everyone was directed straight into the sleeping cars. The arrangements here were quite different to those at home. Bunks ran on either side, up and down the length of the long cars. There were lower and upper bunks, each with an opaque colourless curtain to draw across; the only privacy. The bunks were quite roomy, but we had been allocated only two between the five of us. This was an unforeseen problem. We had been told that children travelled free on the trains but it hadn't been mentioned that this didn't include sleeping accommodation. We had paid the full amount for our journey to Edmonton.

That night Richard slept with Ronald. Michael and wee Ronnie cuddled in beside me. It was a crush. However the children were too tired to notice and slept well. The worst thing, as far as I was concerned, was the heat. It was stifling. There seemed to be no air at all. So many people had warned us how cold it would be in Canada at this time of year, and all that had bothered me so far was the heat. Churchill's words came into my head. "I have worried about many things in my life – most of which have never happened!"

To make matters worse for me, that first night on the train, I was developing a cold. All next day my nose streamed and I couldn't stop sneezing but it didn't spoil my enjoyment of the scenery. With daylight we moved from our sleeping quarters into the daytime cars with their broad central corridors and comfortable seats.

I was fascinated by the clear brilliance of the landscape we trundled past; the incredibly blue sky and the sun dazzling a snow-covered vastness. Every so often a French-type village would appear, each with its own slender church spire and cluster of colourful houses. Now and then we saw a sledge skimming along, pulled by horses. Pictures in my mind from *Out of the Westland* came into focus – flying down the St Lawrence on an ice yacht, riding through the snow on a sleigh, skiing in the mountains – log fires in log cabins.

On the train that day, the Grant family whom we had met on the ship had seats next to ours. They weren't saying much until Mrs Grant happening to look out the window, spotted a horse-drawn sledge. Her voice must have been audible to most of the people in the car. "Good heavens," she said, "just look! – we're back in the middle ages and see that never ending snow! How bleak and barren can you get?!"

I realised that we saw things out of totally different eyes. Ronald didn't say very much at all. He spent much of the time reading a Canadian newspaper he had got at Halifax. Both of us, however, remarked on the relaxed atmosphere of this Canadian train that trundled across the land at no great speed. The children seemed to sense it also and were better behaved because of it. They played happily with other children, running up and down the broad corridors and no one checked them.

With departing day, my voice, affected by the virus, was vanishing also. By the time we reached Montreal it had gone altogether and I could only whisper.

Chapter 3

Travelling Transcontinental

At Montreal we had to change trains and say goodbye to many of our shipboard companions. We felt sad knowing it was unlikely that we should ever see them again. The station was much bigger than the one in Halifax and again very warm. People went about without coats. Ronald led me and the boys to a seat.

"If you can manage to look after the boys for a wee while," he said, "I'll see if I can do anything about the sleeping arrangements for the rest of the journey."

"Yes I'll manage," I said, "but don't be too long."

No sooner had he disappeared into the crowd than the boys, who up till then had been perfectly placid, suddenly woke up and darted off – even Ronnie – all running in different directions. It was as though they realised, all at once, that they were no longer cooped up and must take advantage of the fact. I was feeling very tired and had no voice. I felt helpless. Could they get out of the building and on to the track? I didn't think so but I couldn't be sure. Would they get completely lost in the crowd or get on to the street?

In the desperation of the moment I felt tears run uncontrollably down my cheeks. Suddenly the enormity of my situation overtook me. Not only had I no voice but being almost six months pregnant I found difficulty in speedy movement. Ronald had to get the doctor for me on board ship because I was so very sick. I had begged him not to, to begin with, because I knew the rules were that all woman emigrants had to notify a pregnancy and those who were more than five months were not allowed to sail. I hadn't mentioned mine but at last I agreed to a visit from the ship's doctor. They couldn't put me off the ship in the middle of the Atlantic.

I couldn't hide my condition from the doctor when he came. He was horrified when he found out.

"Did your sponsors not tell you, didn't you read, that passengers are not allowed on this ship over five months pregnant? We have no facilities for premature births."

I had been frightened then, frightened by the suggestion that I could lose the baby. But with the doctor's help and that of nurse and stewards who had done all they could to make things easier for us, I had come through it all right. My doctor back home had tried to persuade me to wait behind until after the baby was born.

"I think what you are doing is ridiculous," he had said. "A fourth baby in such quick succession and you don't even know where you are going. You had a problem with your kidneys last time. From the sound of what you tell me you might land in the middle of a wilderness or in some mountain fastness with no hygiene and Red Indian women at the birth."

Ronald and I had talked it over but we were both adamant that, come what may, we should stick together. Any other way would be more difficult, not less. Being an optimist I told myself I would cross bridges when I came to them, not before. But had we been wrong? Our children were our most precious possessions. Were our difficulties only beginning? What would be the reaction of our sponsors when they found out I was pregnant? For a moment I was paralysed into inaction, only tears coming of their own volition.

A woman in uniform (there were a few about to help immigrants) stopped to ask what was the matter. I whispered my predicament. She assured me that the boys would come to no harm and confidently ran after the two older ones whom I managed to point out to her, whilst I caught up with wee Ronnie.

After they were all gathered round my knees again, I realised how fortunate it was that we had bought them red duffle coats back in Dundee. The bright colour of the coats had made them easily spotted in the crowd.

Soon Ronald was back in charge but with the bunk problem unresolved. It should have been arranged before departure. The authorities could do nothing about it now. We would just have to share two bunks between the five of us all the way to Edmonton. The offer to pay extra made no difference.

"Never mind," I said. "You've done your best. Perhaps it won't be quite so hot tonight."

But I was wrong. On this great train that would cross the Great Canadian Shield, the Prairies, the empty rolling lands of Alberta, and the high Rockies to the Pacific, the bunks were just as hot and cramped. However Ronald and the children slept well and I, with my cold still making breathing difficult, fitfully.

The passengers on this train were rather different to those on the Halifax to Montreal run. Many came from different nationalities. Some were what we called 'real Canadians' – strong-shouldered men dressed casually in checked open-necked shirts and women in jeans. We felt out of place in our British clothes – Ronald especially in his suit, collar and tie.

I noticed that the Canadians never complained about the heat or lack of air and guessed one must get used to it. I did think people looked very pale. Our children were apple-cheeked compared to any Canadian children we saw.

Richard and Michael were reasonably well-behaved. A long train journey seemed to suit them. Also they liked the various visits to the dinette where we got buffet meals that were good and not nearly as expensive as we had been led to believe they would be.

Wee Ronnie was a little more difficult to cope with. He had become very self-assured since leaving home and wanted to visit everyone on the train. A young Canadian couple, Hank and Linda Fremain, in particular took his fancy. He bumped into them, by accident, on the very first morning, as they were coming down the corridor. The man was young with rugged good looks and his wife slender and smart with neat, shining red hair. Perhaps the red hair was the mutual attraction!

"Hi! – how are you?" Linda smiled and bent down to speak to him.

Ronnie said Hi back. In fact after that first introduction to the new greeting, he never stopped using it. Here was a nice easy word that suited him. He made full use of it, going up to everyone and saying Hi with a greater or lesser degree of response.

However, he kept going back to Linda and Hank who had seats near to ours. On the first day, about lunch time, Linda came up to us and said,

"That sure is a cute little boy you've got."

I agreed that cute was the right description. He had a chubby baby face, bright trusting blue eyes and red-gold hair unlike Richard who had blonde hair, that was to grow dark like my own, and Michael with wavy pale brown hair like his Dad's. Wee Ronnie was different all right and at an attractive age. As far as he was concerned there were no dragons in the world. I had to watch that I did not let my love for him become over-protective.

"Would you mind if we took him to lunch with us?" Linda asked.

"Not at all, " I said, "how very kind of you. I am sure he would love it." Father Ronald agreed.

Wee Ronnie spent a lot of time with them on the journey, lapping up the attention that was lavished on him alone – a new experience for him. They took him to various meals. They ate more expensively than we did, lunching in the dining car. Ronnie could have anything he wanted. Toward the end of the journey Linda said to me, "Hank and I are going all the way to Vancouver. We're going to miss your little boy. We'd sure like to adopt him."

"Oh, you can have him," I said in a jocular manner. I was rather proud to think people liked Ronnie so much. I myself thought he was pretty terrific, albeit a little exasperating at times, and was pleased to think that others thought the same.

The days spent in the train, travelling through this vast Siberian-type terrain, passed more quickly than Ronald and I had anticipated. We talked to various people and learned a little about Canada. I liked also, to watch people when I thought they weren't looking, speculating about their lives, sometimes making up stories about them.

There was one young woman in particular, who constantly drew my attention. She was tall, attractive, dressed in service uniform, and obviously travelling alone. It was written all over her that she wanted to remain alone. She looked very sad, never smiled, and quite often her eyes were red with silent weeping. Why, I wondered, what tragedy had overtaken her? However, despite her obvious wishes, she was never left alone for long.

"Just look at them!" said Ronald one afternoon, "like bees round a honey pot. That's the third man in an hour that's had a try at her – not that they ever make any headway, although some are really persistent. I think about every man on the train has been to speak with her and you can see they're all wasting their time."

Sometimes she would disappear into the lady's washroom. There I occasionally found her, sitting by the sink, crying outright and dabbing her eyes with tissues.

We stopped at quite a few stations on the way. At each, passengers left and new ones boarded, especially at the bigger places.

On our last night aboard the train, just as it was growing dark, a family got on from a small wayside station in the middle of nowhere. Ronald and I looked at one another. A spontaneous shiver of fear ran down our spines. They looked poor – very poor indeed. Not only were they badly clad, they also looked undernourished. The children's faces were pinched and grey. So the Canadian West wasn't all golden wheat and guineas after all! We thought it wisest to say nothing.

A source of interest for us during that long journey was looking out of the window, getting to know a little of the topography of our new homeland, but long stretches of time would go past when there was very little new to see. The same scenery would go on and on without apparent change, day after day. The morning after we boarded the train we woke to grey skies, snow and land covered with small fir trees. The following morning we woke to grey skies, snow and small fir trees! It was all very monotonous and rather depressing. This was the Great Canadian Shield – a waste land. There were no villages to speak of and hardly a house. Quite often there were lakes and rivers – all frozen over.

"It's beautiful in summer," a fellow traveller told us but Ronald and I privately thought that even in summer, with all the lakes and rivers shining in the sun, there could be just too much of it. We couldn't imagine people coming here. There were only one or two summer cabins to be seen, fashioned out of logs. At this time of year they looked very bleak and deserted. Some of the names painted above the rough-hewn doors appealed to me, like 'Shoo Fly' and 'Lucky Seven' but I didn't know how prophetic they were to become.

At this time of year, near the railroad track, there was no sign of wildlife. In two days, three black crows were the only birds we spotted. We saw no wild animals at all. There was, however, life at the scattered stations that we passed and sometimes stopped at. Our train, this Prairie Schooner, this ship crossing an almost empty sea of land, was obviously one of the highlights of the day especially in the lonelier places. People came to watch it – Red Indians in parkas and beads, cowhands on horseback, all muffled up to the eyes to keep out the frost. They would come dangerously near to the steel tracks (there was no platform or fencing) and on their sturdy horses, race the train for a short while until it gathered speed. For the first time it began to dawn on me what loneliness meant. Were we also going to this sort of life? I quickly put such thoughts aside.

One morning we woke to the Prairies proper. Perhaps it was because the change was so sudden for us, that the Prairie land was far more eye-catching and interesting than we had expected. The sky was clear unhazed blue and the sun blazed on an endless white baking-board flatness where every so often there was a farm or village to break the monotony of the landscape.

We didn't leave the confines of the train on our journey into the Westland, until we came to Winnipeg. We were told that the train would stop there for a few hours and and we could disembark if we wished. When we arrived, we wrapped the boys up as warmly as we could and ventured out to have a look at the town. We didn't stay long. There was a wind blowing straight from the Arctic. It was so searingly cold that we soon scuttled back to the warm cocoon of the train. Never in our lives had we felt anything like the sting of that wind! We understood now, how easy it would be to get frostbite if we were out for long.

At Saskatoon also, we left the train for a short while. It was late in the evening and the boys were fast asleep. We wrapped up well and left Linda in charge. It was very cold but there was no wind which made it bearable. We liked what we saw of Saskatoon. It looked new and clean, each house was of a different design and colour and bright lights were everywhere.

On the morning of the day we were due to leave the train, we were wakened at half past five. We arrived in Edmonton at 6.30am. All was hustle and bustle. A lot of people were disembarking at this capital city of Alberta. Ronald and I were rather surprised to see Hank and Linda up to bid us farewell, but a far greater shock awaited us when Hank said, "Now, about little Ronnie. We'll get our lawyer to send the adoption papers for you to sign as soon as you send us your address and then we can arrange things further."

"Adoption papers!" Ronald turned to me in alarm. "What on earth is he talking about?"

Linda looked at me tearfully. "But you said . . ."

And then it came back to me in a flash the remark I had made earlier in the train. I had been joking of course but she hadn't taken it as a joke. It hadn't remotely crossed my mind that she would take me seriously.

"Oh I'm sorry Linda." There were tears in my eyes also. "I remember what I said to you but I was joking. Surely you knew I was joking!"

Here we were, thousands of miles from the island of our birth, without the slightest idea of where we would sleep that night.

"Joking!" said Linda. "I do not understand."

Tearfully I explained to Ronald and Hank what had happened. I was in a state of shock. I just couldn't believe that things could happen so casually. I would need to be very careful from now on. We may speak the same language, I thought, but the understanding is quite different. No one at home would have picked up that remark wrongly. Hank and Linda took a desperately disappointed and tearful farewell of Ronnie.

Very early in the morning, in this large warm station in

northern Canada, I clutched my brood to me while Ronald went to announce our arrival. There were lots of people in the station, despite it being so early. They stood or sat in small ethnic groups. Some had found corners where it looked as if they had slept all night and were now breakfasting off sandwiches and flask coffee. I heard one little group beside us in conversation. They were not speaking English and I didn't recognise the tongue. It wasn't French or German. Later I learned that they were probably Ukrainian, Hungarian or Polish people; the tail-end of a vast emigration, half a million or more, from the ramshackle Austrio-Hungarian empire, the Ukraine and central Europe, who in the beginning came as tough peasants in sheepskin coats in the wheat-boom years. Mostly they travelled beyond Winnipeg to settle the frozen lonely Prairies, living the first year, perhaps, in sod huts while waiting for cash returns on their wheat crops to be able to build a frame house.

Ronald was soon back but only to tell us we would have to wait for a couple of hours before we could get any further information. The organiser of immigrants didn't come on duty till eight thirty.

Here we were, marooned thousands of miles from the island of our birth, without the slightest idea of where we would sleep that night. All we knew was that it would be somewhere in Alberta!

Chapter 4

South to Red Deer

Two hours took a long time to pass that winter morning in
Edmonton station. Ronald had been told that when the organiser
arrived he would come to see us. Ronald had pointed out where
we would be.

The children, refreshed after their sleep, showed no ill effects
of having being roused so early. They were happy to be alive
and enjoyed the freedom of running over the smooth tiled floor
which, several acres in size, must have seemed to them to go
on forever. The station, as with the previous stops, was too warm.
I took off the boys' red duffles giving them strict instructions not
to run too far. They tried to make friends with two little boys in a
neighbouring group and even although they had no common
language, they succeeded. It was a strange feeling to be
immigrants among immigrants, few of whom, it would appear,
spoke English. While I waited impatiently for the next stage of
our adventure to begin I took note of these people from different
lands who were to be our fellow countrymen and women. They
were engrossed in their own families and hardly glanced towards
us. I wondered if they knew their destinations or if, like us, they
were completely in the dark of where they would be that night.
There was no way of finding out.

It was about 8.45am when a casually dressed man came
striding purposefully towards us. He introduced himself.

"Hi, I'm Jackson Hunt." He wasted no time. "Welcome to
Alberta. You are to travel a few miles further south this afternoon
to a place called Red Deer. Schulz Muller, the dairy farmer you're
to work for, will be at the station to meet you. Your trunks and
hand luggage will be on the train with you. The rest of your boxes,
crates, etc will follow, but it may take a few days for them to

catch up." He told us the time of the train we were to catch for Red Deer. Everything was neatly arranged.

"Any questions?" he asked briskly. He had the air of a man in a hurry.

There were so many questions we couldn't think of one in particular! Jackson Hunt disappeared back into his office and we were left to put in the morning as best we could. Ronald and I felt both apprehensive and excited. The children felt only excited. We ventured out of the station into the clear frosty air of Alberta's capital city. It looked clean and new with no smoking chimneys to make any sort of veil between the city and the sky. The sidewalks had been cleared of snow. Everywhere there were dirty hard-packed ridges of snow, but embroidering the buildings there was plenty of clean white powder sparkling in the sunlight. It was intensely cold but, unlike Winnipeg, there was no wind. People walked briskly. Large cars whizzed by. Traffic rules had to be observed – no jay-walking was tolerated. Crossing was strictly at the lights and quickly. Here car drivers were the important ones.

The train south for Red Deer left Edmonton at 2pm. I wondered how long it would take to go 'a few miles'. This turned out to be seventy. We left sharply on time and sped along. We looked out the windows and saw huge barren rolling plains criss-crossed at intervals by gravel roads that looked as though they went nowhere in particular. Anxiously I watched the landscape for any sign of farms. There weren't many – only one or two lonely houses, bare and unprepossessing with hardly anything in the way of farm buildings. We passed Leduc where an airport for Edmonton was under construction. At this place enormous reserves of oil and natural gas had been found several years before. We passed Ponoka, a small up-and-coming settlement. By 3pm we were in Red Deer.

We were the only passengers getting off the train. Ronald climbed down first onto the frozen ground and lifted the three boys after him, then held out his hand to help me. The brass bell clanged impatiently and a man came to help us off with our luggage but, apart from this one man, there appeared to be no one else about. For a moment we huddled together recovering from the shock of the cold air after the heat of the train. We felt very small and lost, not knowing quite what to do next. Suddenly we were distracted by two men on horseback, muffled up to the eyes, who galloped up to the railroad track and set off in hot pursuit of the train which was already gathering speed and making that long lonely, desolate hooting that we were to get to know so well. Then a tall handsome, weather-beaten man marched sternly towards us dressed in a thick tartan jacket and cap with a visor peak looking as though he meant business. He didn't appear to be particularly dressed for the weather.

"I'm Schulz Muller," he introduced himself.

He had a polite but rather arrogant manner. He also had a certain informality about him, an odd contradiction. He wasted no time in hustling us all into the large cab of his yellow Dodge truck and threw our luggage into the back. The truck engine had never stopped running. Muller jumped back into the cab and we were off. He said very little and we, too, were tongue tied. I had a funny feeling that we were not the sort of people he had hoped for. To him we must have looked very British and odd. Ronald tried to make some kind of conversation.

"Have you a big dairy?"

"Forty to sixty cows – it depends. They're due to be milked shortly," he said and then, as though he was bestowing some great favour on Ronald,

"Seeing you've had a kinda long journey I won't expect you to help with the milking this afternoon but please be out at 5am for the morning milking."

Ronald agreed and conversation lapsed.

I looked out of the cab window. We passed shining new shops and then streets of bright single-storey timber houses, all different shapes and sizes. I wasn't too disappointed in Red Deer. Like its name, it was pretty. But for all its brightness and newness, there was something inconsequential and unsubstantial about it. It reminded me, more than anything, of a town fashioned from a child's building bricks and dumped in the middle of nowhere. Here things did look smaller but perhaps the size of the landscape we had come through had the effect of making normal size buildings look less than they were. There was one landmark, in particular, that attracted our attention. Mushrooming into the sky, high above the houses, rose a slender structure fashioned from what looked to me like green glass. At the top it fluted out into an onion-shaped dome.

"What on earth is that?" I asked, pointing to the tall tower. Muller took his eyes off the road for a moment to follow my finger.

"That's the water tower," he told us in a Canadian accent that had a slight guttural quality about it, "the largest in Alberta. We sure have trouble with water in these parts." He didn't elaborate and I dropped the subject just as Muller swung dangerously into a large almost empty parking lot and stopped the truck with a sickening screech of brakes. In front of us stood what looked like a giant oblong box, across the top of which was printed in bold red letters, *SAFEWAYS*.

Without switching off the engine, Muller turned to me and said,

"This is the supermarket we use. You'll find you can buy most things here. Get supplies to keep you going for a week. If you don't have any dishes, pots or cutlery with you, get some and don't forget a can opener and an alarm clock. Please be as quick as you can. I'm in a hurry today – the godamn milking machine isn't working properly – Ron, you better stay in the truck to keep an eye on your kids."

I noticed that Ronald's name had already been casually shortened! I mentioned to Muller that we had quite a variety of household things with us but that we had been told our crates would not arrive in Red Deer for a few days. He took no notice at all of this information. I turned to Ronald to ask for some money. He counted out forty dollars.

"Will that be enough?" he asked.

I had no idea and Muller said nothing. I climbed down from the cab, walked carefully over the frozen snow and pushed open the large glass doors. A wind of warm air blew around me as I entered. I stood for a moment, confused; tiredness descending in waves, numbing my brain. What was I to do now? Where did I begin? I had never been inside a supermarket before. The brightness and bigness of it flashed in front of my eyes. Soft music was playing. I felt dizzy. The place was practically empty of people and a girl, standing at the cash desk who had been watching me as I entered, spoke.

"You new here? You look lost."

"Yes," I said, "we've just got off the train."

"You got much to get?" the girl asked kindly.

"Quite a bit."

"Well take one of these." The girl helpfully pulled out a trolley on wheels from a row of others.

"Now," said the girl in a pleasant Canadian accent, "go up and down the aisles and you will find all that you want."

I did as she suggested but my brain was still numb. What a display of goods to choose from! Then the thought of our new boss spurred me into action. First of all the essentials – tea, butter, bread and sugar, then foods that were easy to cook, or needed no cooking at all. Back home I was accustomed to getting a week's supply of groceries at a time, so, once I began to fill the trolley it wasn't so difficult. Besides the food, I chose a cooking pot, a few mugs, plates, cutlery and other utensils – anything I thought we might need. The same girl who helped me when I entered the supermarket was at the cash desk to check me out. She was as kind as before and insisted in pushing the trolley to the truck for me.

"I sure hope you like it here," she said before walking back to the warmth of the store.

In no time at all we were off at full speed. The tarmac of the Red Deer streets ended abruptly and we swung crazily along in the frozen ruts of the broad gravel road. The boys were comparatively quiet, their hands gripping the window ledge, their eyes glued in front of them, obviously enjoying the truck ride more than Ronald or I were.

The setting sun was casting a glorious pink glow on the snow-covered ground and the tall dark spruce trees stood up in grand contrast. Always aware of beauty, even in times of stress, I took it all in through my eyes, my skin, my blood. Optimistically I thought, – Yes! I'm going to like it here. Ronald and Muller were silent.

A long time afterwards, I asked Ronald what his thoughts

were on that journey to our new home. How did he feel at the time?

"Scared," he told me, "not for myself, but for you and the children. Scared of what I'd brought you to. From the moment I saw Muller, there was something I didn't like about him, didn't trust."

Ronald saw reality more clearly than I did. He saw too, below the beauty of the landscape, the coldness, the harshness, the loneliness of the land.

Looking back now I think I know what Schulz Muller's thoughts might have been. We were not the sort of people he had hoped for. He hadn't expected a British family – a slimly-built man, dressed in British clothes, looking more like a teacher, lawyer or businessman, than a farm worker with a wife who, no doubt, would be accustomed to a much better way of life than he could or would be prepared to offer. The last immigrants to work for him had been tough Ukrainian peasants accustomed to hard work, long hours and taking orders. Before coming to Canada, they would have known real hardship and, to begin with at least, would have been satisfied with anything Muller cared to give them.

I knew also he had noticed I was pregnant. I had tried to hide the fact but it was no longer possible. One swift glance in the direction of my stomach told him all he needed to know. His thoughts were probably, She's going to be a problem and not much use as a dairy maid for a while – if at all! That I was to work had not been in the bargain but Muller may not have been aware of that. Nor, perhaps, was he aware of the policy at that time for the Western States. This was to step up the settling of English-speaking people who could read and write in order to redress the balance of the influx of so many sometimes illiterate peasants speaking different languages and having different cultures. These people in the past had been encouraged to leave their own troubled countries with the lure of free land on the uninhabited prairies in the far west. The tendency for them to form colonies establishing, on Canadian soil, their own customs, methods and traditions was worrying to the authorities. The men in power now were anxious to make a unified people living under one flag and owning allegiance to only one – the flag of Canada.

Suddenly we swung round the corner, drove through a grove of spruce trees and approached an attractive house made of logs and built like a Swiss chalet. Muller broke the silence.

"Welcome to Redwoods," he said.

My heart lifted. If this was going to be our house it wasn't too bad – but Schulz didn't stop at the chalet.

"Not far now," he said.

We stopped at the edge of a clump of tall spruce trees. Schulz jumped out the truck indicating that we should do likewise. He then led us down a rough narrow track between the trees and in the twilight we got the first glimpse of the shack we were to inhabit.

Afterwards Ronald confided in me, "When I first saw it I thought it was the outside lavatory!"

His description wasn't far out. What we saw was a rude hovel made out of clapboard, with wooden shingles as roofing. It had a small rickety porch with a distinct list which gave the whole shack the same appearance. Muller scraped open the outside door leading into the porch. It was badly in

"From the moment I saw Muller, there was something I didn't like about him, didn't trust."

need of attention before it fell to pieces. Then he squeaked open the screen door and we entered what we immediately recognised as the kitchen because of the enormous cook-stove that confronted us.

Outside was white dry cold but the moment the porch door was opened we felt a waft of warm air. The stove was lit for our coming although it wasn't the sole supply of heat. Muller showed us, with pride, a small oil heater in the corner of what he called the bedroom. The heat from it radiated through the whole house.

After showing us the heater Muller turned to go.

"I'll leave the truck at the top of the trail so that you folks can

get your things out," he said " . . . must get to that darn milking –
I'm late!"

"Beds," said Ronald as he was about to escape, "what about
beds?"

Apart from the stove and an old couch, the shack was
completely empty. Up till then I think we were both too stunned
to say anything. Beds were the first thought that came into
Ronald's mind before Muller disappeared.

He half turned back and pointed to the old couch – "That
folds down."

"But for the children . . . ?" Ronald continued.

A look of annoyance came over Muller's face – "I'll see if
Maud has any mattresses to spare." With these last few words
he made his escape and we were left to make the best of our
first Canadian home.

Chapter 5

The Shack at Redwoods

At 4am on that first February morning after we arrived at Redwoods, I stepped outside our shack standing all on its own in the very heart of the Westlands. Many coloured curtains of light shifted across the dark bowl of night. Their silent, wide sweeping movements, reminded me of searchlights in wartime. But they had been dull in comparison to these shot-silk waves of brilliance. Moving with a sense of excitement, these Northern Lights, these Merry Dancers, swayed backward and forward and were reflected on a field of virgin snow that stretched on and on beyond the sight of human eye. At intervals, from the rainbow-coloured earth, great orange flames leaped upward like wild demons. Oil had been found here; these flames were manifestations of the burning off of natural gas that would otherwise have exploded underground or spread poisonous fumes into the atmosphere.

The scattered clumps of tall dark spruce trees, alone, were still. I stood in amazement – just looking. Never in my strangest dreams had I imagined or expected such spectacular beauty.

I didn't stand for long. It was intensely cold. With gloved hand I took hold of the freezing cast-iron handle of the pump that stood at the side of the shack. With vigorous movements I jerked it up and down. It was quite some time before any water appeared and when it did it gushed out in great spurts, spilling over the battered kettle's rim and freezing instantly on my shoes.

Then I heard them! They broke the silence like banshees, frightening the night. My heart froze within me. What beasts made so eerie a sound? – Were they hungry? – Had they smelled human flesh? I hurried back into the shack and quickly closed the rickety door.

It was warm inside. Life came back into my heart and limbs. I could feel my cheeks glowing. The oil heater in the corner of the boys' bedroom gave off a steady glow. Heat came also from the cast-iron cook-stove which I had banked up with green logs (the only fuel provided) before going to bed. It wasn't quite out. I poked it. It spluttered into life. Slowly flames began to curl round the fresh logs. I placed the kettle on the fire. It was a very old one and had a small leak in the bottom which caused the hotplate to hiss and spit at regular intervals. I heard a movement coming from the couch behind me and a voice, thick with sleep, saying,

"My God! where am I?"

He must have remembered because his next words were, "I didn't hear you get up."

"I've been up for ages," I boasted. "I've been out getting water from the pump."

Ronald slipped out of the couch-come-bed and put on the clothes he had laid out the night before. The kettle boiled more quickly than I expected and I made two cups of coffee, then poured the rest of the water into the pot I had bought at the supermarket, to make porridge.

"So much for the great Canadian welcome people kept telling us about," said Ronald looking about him.

"Well," I agreed, "it certainly hasn't been up to much so far, but worse than that, when I was out at the pump, I heard the most fearsome howling. Do you think it might be wolves?"

"The Mullers would have warned us of any danger. It's more likely to be coyotes and they're reputed to be harmless."

I left the subject and came up with the next thing on my mind.

"This morning it's beautiful outdoors. The sky is alive with colour – Northern Lights – like those back home but much much brighter and more colourful. Also there are fires everywhere – great flames leaping up into the sky. It's not really dark outside at all."

Ronald was in no mood to talk about such things.

"We can't stay here for long, beautiful or not. This shack really is the pits but we'd better stick it for a wee while – try to find our feet. We can't go further just yet." He took a gulp of hot coffee.

"If this is what they call a furnished house, I'd hate to think what an unfurnished one is like!"

Ronald was right. All that the shack contained, when we arrived, was the dilapidated couch (a Winnipeg couch, Maud Muller had called it) on which we had spent the night, an old black kettle that leaked, an ancient mop and bucket, a brush of the witches broom variety, the big black stove and the oil heater. There was also a sink of sorts but no plumbing.

About half an hour after Shultz Muller introduced us to the cabin Maud Muller came to the door dragging an old mattress behind her through the snow.

"For the children," she said

Ronald had helped her into the shack with it and then went up to the top of the track to get another one out of the truck.

Our new home was divided, by slim partitions, into three parts. The main kitchen-cum-livingroom took up one half. The other half was cut down the middle to make two small square rooms. In one of them stood the oil heater. It was here we had put the two mattresses for the boys and the fold-down pram that we had

I stood in amazement – just looking. Never in my strangest dreams had I imagined or expected such spectacular beauty.

brought with us for Ronnie. They had all slept deeply. Even now, with all the movement and talk in the main room, they remained totally undisturbed. Ronald and I didn't have much time for further discussion. He ate the breakfast I had made for him and departed just before 5am, not wanting to be late.

After he had gone I got to work in the cabin. First I made up the couch, then got more water from the pump to fill up the boiler at the side of the stove. I then brought in an armful of freezing logs from the wood-pile. When the water was hot I washed up the morning's dishes, also those I had left from the night before. The sink ran out into a bucket. I noticed a thin trickle of water on the bare wood floor. The bucket obviously leaked as well as the kettle, so I hastily took it and threw the dirty water outside the cabin. It made a nasty stain on the snow.

I was still tired. I hadn't slept well. From the moment I lay down a tooth had begun to ache. Now, with the aid of aspirins, it was beginning to feel a bit better.

The boys woke up as daylight crept through the window. Soon sunlight flooded the cabin. I looked out on an enchanted land of white snow. Here and there the dark contrast of vertical spruce trees broke the horizontal whiteness. Above, the sky was speedwell blue. Lost in a greater light than theirs, the burning flames, so brilliant a few hours ago, were now almost invisible. It was impossible to be downhearted.

The children couldn't wait to get outside. I was cautious. It was cosy in the house, but I knew how cold it was beyond the wooden door. I wrapped them up as warmly as I could and pushed open the screen door leading into the porch. On the ledge that ran above us round the porch something moved and caught the corner of my eye. I looked more closely and a bright eye, trusting and round as a rowan berry, looked straight into mine. My heart gave a jump of delight.

"Look boys," I said, pointing upwards.

The creature quickly and with agility, moved to the farthest dark corner. It took the boys a moment or two before they saw it.

"Mummy, Mummy, what is it?" Richard said in an excited voice.

"It's a squirrel of some kind," I said in a sort of hushed awe anxious not to scare it away. "Isn't it pretty?"

It was a handsome creature, rather like the Scottish squirrel but larger. It had a glossy coat and a gloriously bushy tail. It didn't seem to be at all in awe of us and not a bit frightened. It became one of our very few friends in this, our first Canadian home.

I went out with the boys into the sunlight. We walked up the narrow trail and heard hammering sounds amongst the spruce trees – the busy beaks of woodpeckers searching for food. From the top of the trail one could see for a long way. I stretched my eyesight to the outer limits looking for another dwelling. Apart from the Muller's log cabin, there was nothing – absolutely nothing! I wondered if our nearest neighbours lived in the Indian reserve which, Muller had mentioned, started several miles away.

"There are two Indian reserves near here," he had said while driving us to Redwoods.

This morning his words, more real now, came back to me. My goodness! I thought. Perhaps we are surrounded by Indians.

At twelve noon Ronald came in for a quick lunch. Muller had said he could have an hour off at midday, but Ronald thought he had better not take so long, as there was still a lot to do in the dairy. I didn't see him again till eight that evening.

Chapter 6

Taking Stock

On the second evening at Redwoods, it wasn't until after we had our picnic tea from a cloth spread on the bare boards of the kitchen floor, and the boys were tucked up for the night, that Ronald and I had time to take stock of our position. Looking on the bright side, we both agreed that at least we had shelter, were warm and had enough to eat. When Maud Muller had delivered the mattresses, the previous evening, she had said to me, before rushing off into the night,

"I go into Red Deer every morning with the milk at 7am. On Tuesdays I get groceries from the store as soon as it opens. On that day you can come with me and get what you need." Then she had disappeared like a wraith.

Maud Muller was a small woman and gave the impression of fragility which must have been erroneous. Her quick movements reminded me of nothing so much as an over-anxious bantam. Beneath this exterior I sensed a kindness that she had to keep cooped up.

Ronald now settled down more comfortably into the couch.

"How are you going to get to a doctor or a dentist?" he asked anxiously.

"Don't worry about that," I told him, "I'll mention it to Mrs Muller on Tuesday."

Ronald, looking on the bright side, remarked,

"The kids seem happy enough."

"Yes they are," I said. "They really are. They enjoyed themselves today. They like the novelty of picnics on the floor and sleeping on mattresses. Kids are versatile. They don't need much to be happy. As long as we don't make too much fuss about things, they'll accept almost anything and, of course, as long as we love them."

Ronald agreed with this piece of unexpected philosophy. We turned our discussion to our new home.

"It's remarkably warm," Ronald said.

"I've discovered one of the reasons," I said. "Look," I pointed to the small square curtainless window – "a touch of class here – pink toilet paper!"

All round the frame of the window, where it had been fitted into the wall, tissue had been stuffed into the cracks. Ronald laughed. In fact, everywhere we looked – wherever there was the slightest crack or cranny, toilet paper had been neatly squeezed in to act as insulation. No finger of frost could poke its way in anywhere.

"There's no running water or plumbing," Ronald continued. "I suppose we might have expected that, but there's no table or chairs and we were promised a furnished house."

"When our boxes come, the large one can be used as a table, the two smaller ones as benches," I suggested, "until we get something better."

Ronald's eye now fell on the stove that was crackling away merrily in spite of green logs.

"That sure is some stove," he said. "The only time I have seen anything like it before was in a Western."

"And it works!" I said. "These big thin steel pipes throw out the heat and boy! are they ever hot! Fortunately they're above the reach of the children. And that long hob would take a lot of pots if we had a lot of pots to put on it, and the water compartment, at the end of the stove heats really quickly. Look at the size of the bread oven. You could bake enough for an army in it."

Ronald laughed, glanced at my inelegant figure and said,

"At this rate we'll need it!" Then he took to speculating, "It will be good if we have a little girl this time, but another boy would be OK. How proud I would be to have four sons!"

I drew closer to him on the couch and gave him a hug. Ronald broke the silence in a matter of fact manner.

"The lavatory leaves a lot to be desired."

"Yes," I said.

It stood among the spruce trees at the back of the house and was small, dark and freezing.

"There's one thing," I said, "there won't be many germs about at this time of year! That's about the only good aspect of the little house that I can think of."

"And there really is a 'can' at the door!" Ronald laughed. "I'd heard about 'life in the backwoods' but I don't think I quite believed it until now."

Once we'd stopped laughing, Ronald left the subject and turned his attention to the electricity. The wiring was in a bad way and the switches temperamental. It had been hastily and badly put in and none too recently. Ronald was more aware of the danger than I was. I felt that our lives were in the hands of God anyway and being of an optimistic nature, that God was kind. Here I could have been quite wrong. Many shacks went on fire in the backwoods. Fortunately for my peace of mind, I wasn't aware of this at the time.

The days that followed were, for me, a time of isolation. I got no encouragement to go and speak to Mrs Muller and she didn't come near me. Ronald was away long hours. There was no telephone, radio or postman. I would have welcomed a visit from a curious Indian, but there was no one.

Then one afternoon, about two weeks after our arrival, a little ordinary lady, warmly furred and neatly hatted, sailed down the track. She seemed to come from nowhere and was a member of the tribe 'Jehovah's Witness'. Firmly clasped to her ample bosom, she carried copies of the inevitable *Watchtower*. Jehovah himself could not have got a bigger welcome! She came to me as a saviour, although not the kind she had in mind. I asked her to sit on the Winnipeg couch, gave her tea and biscuits and plied her with questions about our new unknown world called Canada. Somewhat stunned and subdued, she answered my questions politely, as best she could, and handed me a *Watchtower*, her trademark, in exchange for some cents and then left.

In those two weeks, apart from the night we arrived, I had seen Maud Muller only once, and that was early on Tuesday morning when she took me into Red Deer in the Dodge to get groceries. She was in a hurry. Later, I was to discover that many people in Alberta seemed perpetually to hurry. The light air and the influence of so much sunshine maybe had something to do with it. Here, on this high plateau, although we didn't appear to be anywhere near elevated ground, we were actually living 3,000 feet above sea level. Here, the air was rarer.

That early Tuesday morning, we bowled along the gravel road at considerable speed, with Mrs Muller, myself and three sleepy boys in the cab of the yellow Dodge truck, milk cans swaying in the back. Half way to Red Deer I summoned up courage to ask if there was a dentist in the town.

"We have everything in Red Deer," she answered with considerable pride.

"I have a tooth that is very painful. Would it be possible to get it out?"

"I'll make an appointment for you," she said. "Leave it to me."

She volunteered no further information and I left it at that. I didn't mention doctor. I thought one at a time was enough. To give Mrs Muller her due, I felt she would have liked to have said and done more to help. She looked tired. Her hair was mousey and plain. Her weathered brow more furrowed than it should have been for someone I guessed would be in her late thirties. Her rather delicate hands were rough, coarsened by work and weather, her grey eyes noncommittal and weary. It was hard to imagine a smile from her colourless lips. I guessed she was frightened of her Germanic husband – didn't dare cross him.

I learned later that life on the land was tough for everyone here. If we thought we had a hard luck story, it was minor beside many we came to hear about. People just didn't complain. Maud Muller never mentioned that several years ago her home had been burned down and that they had lived for two years in the hen house until they built their chalet with their own hands.

On the way home Mrs Muller announced, "I've made an appointment for you at the dentist at 8.30 on a Tuesday morning." She mentioned a date a month further on.

"A whole month!" I couldn't help remonstrating. "In Scotland, if you're in much pain, a dentist will take you right away."

"They don't here," she said.

51

I could see the subject was closed. Little else was said on the homeward journey in the truck that rattled more now that the milk cans were empty. She did throw out the information, however, that everyone around these parts had some sort of vehicle of their own but gave no hint as to how the purchase of such a necessity could be accomplished. In fact she quickly closed the subject before I could say, "But how?"

One evening, after we had been at Redwoods for several weeks, when the children were fast asleep and we were sitting on our one and only seat-come-bed in front of the log stove, Ronald came out with,

"Muller is keeping me prisoner here. I don't know what his game is and I don't like it. I expected hard work when I came to Canada but this goes over the score. Five in the morning till seven at night with hardly a break for a meal and only a Sunday afternoon off. What kind of hours are these and all for a pittance. Plus he's hinted that my hours will be longer when the Spring sowing starts. That I'm getting it easy now. And he's a bully, although I don't take too much notice of that. I can handle it but what I can't stand is that young son of his who looks in, from time to time, when he's off school and tells me what to do in the same hectoring manner as his father."

"How old is he?"

"Oh about sixteen – little whipper snapper in his German hat – going to be just like his old man."

Ronald was tired, worried and angry, his usual humour which made the world a brighter place had vanished. I knew his pride was severely dented by Muller's son whom I never actually saw. My lot was easy compared with his. I knew how difficult it must be for him to take these kinds of orders. Doubly so after being his own boss for so long and from a schoolboy!

Something had to be done – but what? We were in a difficult position – far from anywhere – no contact with the outside world – not even able to get to a phone. The thought of writing to the immigration people was difficult. Whining already, they would probably say, although surely their standards were higher than this. We had been promised a furnished house and no way could anyone call this shack furnished. Besides, there was nowhere I knew of to post letters. I would have to give them to Maud Muller. She would see the CNR address and guess it might mean trouble – would she post it? – would it make things harder for Ronald?

Very unexpectedly, towards the end of the fourth week, Muller briskly announced to Ronald,

"Tomorrow is Saturday – you can have a half day off."

When Ronald came in at lunch time he told me the good news and added,

"I'll go to Red Deer tomorrow."

"How?" I asked.

"Walking."

"You can't possibly – not at this time of year. It's twenty miles or more. It will be dark before you get there and you know how dramatically the temperature drops once the sun goes down. And what's more, you don't have proper clothes for sub-zero temperatures."

"I know – that's one reason I need to go. I'll have to work outside soon, on the land. I haven't the proper clothing and Muller offers nothing. I must do something. You told me that Maud Muller said most stores stay open late on a Saturday in Red Deer and that's when the people from the 'sticks' do their shopping."

"Muller is keeping me prisoner here. I expected hard work when I came to Canada but this goes over the score."

"Yes she did say that when she told me about most people having cars."

"Walking to Red Deer is a risk I've got to take," Ronald said. "I know the dangers and I mean to keep walking till I get there but what I'm counting on is a passing motorist giving me a lift once I get to the main drag. I'm told they don't pass someone walking. They know how dangerous it can be in winter."

Ronald's mind was made up. I knew I could not alter it.

"I'll leave as soon as I get off work tomorrow. Have some

53

sandwiches ready for me and lay out my warmest, most windproof clothes."

Ronald finished work next day at twelve o'clock and by twelve thirty the children and I walked with him to the top of the winding path. He gave us all a hug and promised the boys he would bring them back something from Red Deer if they were good and looked after me. We stood for a while in the bright sunshine to give him a last wave as he disappeared through a clump of tall pine trees and then scuttled back to the warmth of the of the wood stove and the most apprehensive afternoon of my life.

Chapter 7

Beyond the Bright Snowfields

Ronald must have looked a very odd sight that cold afternoon in the middle of the huge Canadian landscape. He lacked the proper clothing for winter in Alberta but had dressed up as best he could in what he had – long johns beneath the trousers of a tweed suit and as many of my hand-knitted jumpers as would go on under his long camel coat. The tweed trilby that suited his handsome features was useless for this climate as it did not protect his ears. It was now clamped down with my warmest woollen scarf tied round his chin. I had awful visions of something I had once read. A man had gone walking in sub-zero temperatures with nothing to protect his ears. They had got so cold that he had covered them with his hands. His fingers swelled to enormous proportions, went blue and numb and had to be amputated because of frostbite. To complete the outfit Ronald wore gloves and wellington boots pulled on above two pairs of woollen socks. Although it was now almost March we were going through a cold snap. It was colder than when we first arrived.

Later, after much questioning, I got an accurate picture from Ronald of all that happened after he left us.

At one point along the trail he was too hot so he took off his camel coat and removed one of the jumpers which cracked with static electricity in the dry frozen air. He walked on for miles along the white track, happy to be free at last. Fortunately there had been no fresh falls of snow and the track was easy to follow because of the tyre marks of Muller's Dodge. Coyotes loped across his path incredibly close to him and once, in the distance, he saw a moose, its dark body and huge horns well-defined against the snow-covered land. At one point on the road he saw something more menacing – the unmistakable footprints of a bear crossing the track from one clump of trees to another. So there were bears around – Muller hadn't said!

The silence was immense – the only sounds were the rattle of the Whiskey Jacks and the rat-tat-tat of the woodpeckers when he passed a clump of pines. Eventually he came to the highway – a wide gravel road, its deep ruts stretching far into the distance. At first he felt elated walking along it, sandy gravel showing through the rutted snow. Soon, he thought, a truck or car will pass and give me a lift. But there was nothing – only snow and silence and the endless road going straight to the horizon. The constant walking in bright glare began to affect his eyes (we had brought no sun glasses with us) and he had to walk with his gloved hands shading his face. After a while his arms grew tired in that position. By the time the sun began to sink Ronald began to suffer from exhaustion. The last few weeks of work had been tiring in themselves plus living at a much higher altitude than he was accustomed to had taken its toll. Back home our farm, tucked into a fold in the hills, was no higher than five hundred feet. It took a while to get acclimatised to the change. On top of it all was the long walk in the dazzling light.

He kept his spirits up by whistling tunes of home into the empty air and thinking about the town beyond these snowfields – Red Deer with its proper houses, its shops and most of all its people. He would get talking to someone, surely, who would be able to help with advice if nothing else. Eventually, however, sleep began to seem very attractive. He knew he must not give into this. In falling temperatures to sit down and close his eyes could prove fatal. He trudged on in a sombulant state, hands mercifully released at last from having to constantly shade his eyes.

Now the wide earth had become a glorious shade of pink. He stopped for the hundredth time to look behind and listen. Tired though he was he could not help but marvel at the enormous pink landscape taking its reflection from a spectacular red sky. Was that a flurry of pink on the horizon? He couldn't be sure. He was beginning to imagine things. Was this the Arctic equivalent of a mirage in the desert and was the noise he heard the throb throb throbbing of his exhausted heart. The flurry of pink grew greater and the noise louder, becoming a low roar. A vehicle was approaching, fast now through a spume of pink snow – it didn't appear to be slowing down. Quickly Ronald came out of his sombulance and dramatically flagged it down, his long arms flailing the frozen air. They must see him – They must!! The truck skeetered to a halt. The window opened and the moon-shaped face of the driver appeared.

"You going far? You sure look plum tuckered out."

That evening, several hours after darkness had fallen, Ronald still hadn't come back. For a few minutes I turned my back on the warm shackful of high-spirited children with strict instructions to Richard to look after his brothers. I opened the rickety door and stepped out into the night hurrying through the spruce trees to the top of the path. A three-quarter moon was climbing up the enormous sky throwing over the silent wilderness a strange blue luminance. To the north, at the rim of night, the sky appeared to be trembling where tentative rays of swaying light were stretching out, falling back, colour coming and going as it does in a rainbow – fading, fixing, fading, fixing. Tonight, because of the fear in my heart for Ronald's safety, I saw the cold unearthliness as well as the beauty. I felt very small and alone. Even the

At one point he saw something more menacing – the unmistakable footprints of a bear crossing the track from one clump of trees to another. So there were bears around!

burning brands of natural gas had lost all warmth and appeared as red-gold mythical birds escaping the earth. In the distance I again heard the eerie howling of the coyotes although I now knew I had nothing to fear from them. We had seen them in the day time loping across the snow away from us until, curiosity getting the better of the little fear they had, they would stop to look back and ponder at our presence in their land. To us they looked like pale Alsatian dogs. Tonight they were invisible – just a host of uncanny sounds. I strained my ears to hear any other noise but there was nothing – just a vast lonely silence.

I trundled back down the path and stepped into the relative security of the shack. There was plenty of noise in the kitchen. Michael and Ronnie were fighting over a toy car and Richard trying to keep the peace. Richard broke away from the other two and ran over to me.

"Did you see Daddy coming?" he said.

"No, darling, perhaps he'll be a wee while yet. Let's have supper."

Soon we were picnicking on the floor in comparative silence. Not long after we had finished and before I had time to clear up, we heard the unmistakable tooting of a truck horn. Excitedly we rushed to the small square window. Richard and Michael were just tall enough to see out of it. I took Ronnie in my arms so that he could see out also.

"It will be Daddy. It's sure to be Daddy," I said confidently.

At first all we saw was the empty path patterned by moonlight and then a tall man hurrying down. He looked different to the one we had waved goodbye to earlier in the day. At first the boys didn't recognise him dressed as he was in a Canadian quilted jacket complete with fur-lined hood and large snow shoes on his feet. He looked like someone coming home from an Arctic expedition. Ronald wasn't alone. Behind him came a couple who looked of an age with ourselves and a small child. I rushed to the door to scrape it open and let Ronald and the strangers in.

"Hi," said the strange man without waiting for an introduction. "I'm Bill and this is my wife Mary and daughter Tracy. We met up with Ron on our way into Red Deer – strange apparition we spotted in front of us – you sure wear funny clothes over in the old country. He sure looked tired, had been walking for ages. We gave him a lift – helped him to get a few things."

"Thank you so much," I said, relief flooding through me. I

invited the strangers in and gave Ronald a big hug while the children clambered round him. I offered them supper but Bill said they had all eaten at Red Deer not long ago. I offered a coffee which they accepted. The kettle was boiling on the hob and soon they were all cradling cups of coffee in their cold hands.

"A biscuit," I said handing round a plateful.

"Thanks," said Bill. "We call them cookies over here."

I laughed. "It'll take me a while to become a Canadian."

I gave Tracy a drink of orange juice along with the boys and Richard offered sweets from the large packet Ronald had given them. She accepted politely and sat quietly by her mother. I saw Bill and Mary giving furtive looks round our cabin.

"Ron's been telling us about the predicament you're in," Bill said after a while. "But I think you gotta see it to believe it. We've always known Muller was mean but this sure takes the cookie – you've nothing!" he said. I saw him looking at the remains of our picnic on the floor.

"This guy's no good – hasn't many friends. Several years ago his house burnt down. They put a notice in the paper when they started to build their new one. It's done in these parts. Usually the neighbours all come to help out but they didn't this time. He'd just been so god-darned mean to people. They lived in a henhouse for two years, served them right – he just doesn't give a shit for folk. She's not so bad but doesn't mix much – afraid of him they say. People are kinda sorry for her but there's not much anyone can do." Bill was silent for a moment before veering on to our present day problems.

"Trouble is," he said, "it sure is tough for immigrants. You tend to get the bad bosses, those that no one else will work for. Now take my boss. He's not bad – pay's not all that good but he treats us well – goes off to Oregon in the winter leaving me in charge. We live about ten miles down the trail from you folks – similar sort of place but no dairy – that's a killer."

Bill and Mary taught us a lot that evening about the sort of life we had so unwittingly entered into. They also told us about themselves.

"I'm Canadian," Bill said proudly. "My father was Welsh and my mother Latvian but I was born and raised here."

Bill looked Welsh. Stockily built he had dark wavy hair and a cheerful expression. Mary was also proud of being born Canadian.

"My people are Russian," she told me, "but I had an Irish stepfather."

By the time the Joneses rose to go Tracy had fallen asleep beside her mother on the Winnipeg couch. Mary woke the sleeping child to bundle her up in her parka. Bill carried her to the truck.

"I'll be back tomorrow," he said as he went out the door.

Bill did come back the next day laden with various household goods that he and Mary thought might be useful. He also brought a pile of Canadian magazines, two loaves of bread, a chocolate cake baked by Mary and a jar of jam which had a strange sweet flavour I didn't recognise. The next time I saw Mary I asked her what berries she had used to make the jam.

"Saskatoons," she told me. "They grow wild around here. We gather them in summer."

One of the most useful things Bill brought that day was an old iron. I would have to use the floor as an ironing board but it was better than nothing. That afternoon Bill insisted that I and the children should go to town with him to get what we needed. Ronald had had only enough time to get a few necessities in Red Deer before the stores had closed. I didn't like the idea of putting Bill out of his way but it didn't take much persuasion for me to accept the offer. He took me to the store in Red Deer where goods were cheapest and with his helpful advice I bought two water pails, a kettle and a boiler. The latter was a big galvanised container that would fit along the entire length of the stove. To my surprise it cost only three dollars. It looked as if it would have cost more. It was to come in very useful indeed as water heater, wash tub and bath for the boys.

After the purchase of the hardware, Bill took me where I could buy clothes for the children. Mostly everything I had brought from Scotland was woolly or contained a percentage of wool. This was excellent for keeping at bay the damp cold of my native land but was wrong for the intensely dry cold climate of Alberta. Here wool was uncomfortable to wear and showered off sparks of static electricity. I bought the boys padded cotton parkas with fur-trimmed hoods, small replicas of the one Ronald had bought for himself and waterproof snowboots that went over their shoes. There was one other thing I needed to get before leaving Red deer – a radio for Ronald. He wanted one in order, as he put it, to keep in touch with the outside world. Bill led me to another shop and carefully examined all the radios on offer. Suddenly he pounced.

"Now look at this one," he said. "Only twelve dollars. This sure is a bargain." He looked really pleased with his find. There was no greater joy in Bill's life than to stumble on a bargain, whether for himself or someone else.

We bought the radio and that concluded the purchases. The boys by this time were beginning to get impatient. Dressed in their new parkas and snowboots, they were in a hurry to get home to show Dad what they had got. Bill collected our crate and boxes from the station. They had been there for some time to be collected but Muller had never made the slightest move to get them for us. We made for Redwoods as darkness was falling.

Everything we bought that day proved useful. Life became a little easier. Even the children's new clothes, apart from being warmer and more comfortable for them, saved me effort and it was possible to let them run in and out of the shack without spending so much time wrapping them up. The snowboots were a great boon. I trained the boys to remove them in the porch before coming in to the kitchen. Previously they just ran out and in with their shoes on and sometimes, when I wasn't looking, came in and went through to their bedroom where they danced on the blankets of their makeshift beds with them on. Sometimes the soles of their shoes were black with oil.

"You know," said Ronald one day not long after we arrived, "I'm sure this shack must sit on an oil well."

As soon as the sun melted the snow or earth round the door, the ground oozed oil to harden again when the sun went down. Alberta, we were later to discover, was rich in many minerals including oil.

Chapter 8

The Little Old House on the Prairie

The days passed happily enough for the children in that first month in Alberta. We tried not to show them our anxiety. From time to time, I was also happy in spite of everything. The constant sunlight had a lovely effect. In the afternoons I went out with the boys. We would wander along in our new snow shoes, and see the coyotes loping across the snow and the bright plumaged woodpeckers among the trees, their persistent drilling of pine trunks making a rapid staccato sound.

We also came across, now and again, signs of another drilling – drilling for oil. Small pumps for all the world like huge woodpeckers dancing up and down. Sometimes the boys would play in the sandy ruts where the snow had melted on the trail. We never however, remained outdoors for any length of time. It was too cold.

On the day Bill Jones took us to Red Deer he also gave us an invitation.

"Mary told me," he said, "to ask you folk to our place for a meal one evening after Ronald's finished work. We'd sure like to have you. Would you like to come?" He need hardly have asked.

Bill came for us the following Wednesday at 7pm sharp. We all bundled into the cab of his truck, the children sitting on our knees. We drove several miles along a gravel road with no sign of habitation anywhere. All of a sudden we stopped.

"I'd sure like to show you folks somethin'," Bill said.

We all scrambled out. It was very cold outside the heated cab and we walked off the track a bit, following Bill through an area of pine trees. Climbing through snow, we clambered up a steep slope and without any warning found ourselves looking down into a tremendous valley. Not a dead valley but one very much alive, dancing with the lights of several townships. Everywhere, from the burning off of natural gas, leaping flames wavered upwards. We could also see the dim outlines of one or two delicate masts like the riggings of a ship with sails furled. I pointed in their direction.

"What are these?" I asked Bill.

"Television masts," he told me.

So we weren't so far from civilisation after all.

"Look further," Bill said.

We strained our eyes and by the light of the rising moon could just make out, on the western horizon, a great barrier, rugged and remote – the Rocky Mountains.

We retraced our steps and all bundled into the truck again bumping and swaying along the rough rutted road for a few more miles. Bill's cabin was hidden among trees at the top of an incline. By the time we reached it, the moon had risen sufficiently to allow it to sparkle on the snow and shine on the house in the clearing. The night air was light, dry, cold. The cabin looked like something in a dream. It was constructed from the same kind of wooden slats as our own but had been freshly painted which gave it a much better appearance. It looked a little odd, unreal, perhaps, alone in the middle of nowhere.

All unreality left, however, as soon as we entered and felt the warm air and the even warmer welcome of our gentle hostess. Mary was a delicate girl, small-boned with soft brown hair and dark brown eyes. She did not look the sort of person one would find in a wilderness and, disappointingly for me, she didn't look Russian. Not that I really knew what Russians looked like but she was not as I imagined them to be. Bill was very proud of her. She had literary leanings, he told us on the first night that we met, and he had bought her a typewriter.

Tracy was at the door to welcome us also, jumping with excitement at having company. We were shown into the kitchen-cum-livingroom which, like ours, ran the whole length of the house. In complete domination of the room stood a large antique cook-stove similar to our own. Unlike our kitchen the walls were painted a cheerful yellow. Brown linoleum tiles covered the floor.

On the far wall hung a guitar and a broad-brimmed stetson. The curtains on the two square windows were of white muslin, crisp and fresh. They were looped back with wide yellow bows of the same material and from the pelmet a similar bow hung throwing down two long yellow streamers. Round the walls of the room stood a washing machine, a gigantic fridge and two small tables, one holding a sewing machine and the other the precious typewriter. In the middle of the room two tables had been placed end to end making one big table. It was nicely set with a lace tablecloth and crammed with food. It would have been impossible to get another thing on to it. Mary must have spent a considerable time preparing for our visit.

We ate soon after we arrived. I think Mary noticed that our children couldn't stop looking at the food. Many of Mary's recipes had been learned from her Russian mother. First she put down in front of us steaming plates of borsch, red in colour from all the beetroot used. It tasted wonderful. Then we had ample helpings of beef, simmered long on the black stove. With the beef she gave us roast potatoes and cabbage rolls – large leaves of cabbage spread with savoury rice then folded carefully and again simmered on the stove. What the boys liked best, however, was Mary's chocolate cake. I was a little ashamed of how much they ate of it. Mary, loving children, was indulgent towards them. She also gave them chocolate milk, cold from the fridge. They immediately liked it. Mary told me how to make it and from then on I had no problem getting them to drink milk. We had coffee to finish with. She apologised for not having tea.

"We don't drink tea much around here," she said. "Because the water here ain't all that good. It doesn't mix well with tea. Coffee disguises the taste of it." From then on we kept to coffee ourselves.

I ate so much that I was a little ashamed of myself but I wanted to sample everything – all the things I have mentioned, plus pancakes with maple syrup and homemade bread with Saskatoon jam. Mary looked pleased that her efforts were so much appreciated. We began to remember what civilisation was like.

After the meal we sat round the stove and talked while Tracy took the boys through to her room to play with her toys.

"You're a beautiful baker," I said to Mary.

"You'll find most Canadian women are," she said, "even in the towns. It's the flour. It's light – easy to bake with. Many bake their own bread. We used to have to – so far from stores. Now we've all these new supermarkets but we haven't lost the habit yet, I guess. I still cook the old-fashioned way. Many of my recipes are Russian from my mother or Irish from my stepfather but many women, especially in the towns, work now and buy ready-cooked meals. Things are sure changing."

After a while Mary went off to see what the kids were up to. They were amazingly quiet. While she was out of the room Ronald said,

"Your home is very well equipped. You've got everything you could wish for here."

"Well I sure like to give Mary things. She appreciates them so much. She had some god-damn childhood with a stepfather that beat her and always they had to struggle with poverty. They all had to work very hard to make ends meet at all. They had nothing. Even their curtains were of sackcloth, their cabin unpainted."

Mary came back with the children following her. Bill moved over to the far wall and took down his guitar and played and sang to us. The songs he chose were mostly Westerns like *The Green, Green, Grass of Home, The Blue Tail Fly,* and *Home on the Range*. Ronald and I joined in when we knew the words.

All good evenings come to an end sooner or later, and this one did when wee Ronnie could not keep his eyes open any longer and fell asleep on my knee.

Bill drove us back. The moon was now directly overhead. I had expected to see the Northern Lights in all their glory, but not tonight. Perhaps the moon was too bright. Their presence was there however, the night pulsating palely with their movement like a great cold heartbeat. But within us we felt no coldness, only warmth for these complete strangers, born of a different people, who were doing so much to help us.

Another form of contact for us now was the radio. It was not however, quite the contact with the outside world Ronald had hoped for. Reception was none too good and the stations we tended to get were local. The people running them gave the impression that there was very little news outside their area and what there was was of minimal importance. I felt that had an atomic bomb dropped on, say, Toronto, the information would have come at the end of the news and no one would have bothered much about it.

There was though, some preoccupation with an atom bomb coming straight from Russia across the 'Dew Line' (the early warning system in the far north) and dropping on Edmonton, the first city of any size it would encounter. Apart from local news, advertisements, and the name of Alberta repeated often and importantly, there was little else on it other than music. The latest hit song was played at ten minute intervals until one was truly sick of it. Once a week Alberta's Prime Minister came on the air. Premier Manning ran a religious programme and would start off by telling his listeners,

"This is Premier Manning speaking to you from your old-fashioned 'Back to the Bible Hour'."

Towards the end of the programme he would say to his listeners,

"Now wherever you are, stand up and shake everyone by the hand, whether you know them or not."

I felt like shouting back, "But there's no one here to shake hands with!"

One night when we had sat up a little later than usual and Ronald was fiddling about with the knobs on the radio, we came across, very faint and far away, another station. We heard a low voice say,

"This is Salt Lake City."

How exciting and mysterious. Salt Lake City – back home this would have seemed a mythical place – unreachable. It proved to be the most distant station we could find and we were only able to tune in late at night.

A closer kind of contact began to filter in to us with the arrival of letters. Muller passed them to Ronald who brought them in at lunchtime. I had written quite a few not long after we arrived to let friends and relations know our new address. I gave them to

Maud Muller to post for me when she came for us on Tuesday mornings. My mother was the first to reply. Her letter was full of hope, praise and encouragement which was what we needed more than anything else. Ronald's father wrote and other relatives from Scotland telling us what had happened there since we left. They all helped us to feel that the links with home were not completely broken.

Then I got a letter with the postmark, Toronto. I knew the handwriting. Sheila and I had been close friends from nursing days and had both put our names down for work in a hospital in Kenya when our training had finished. But I had got married and Sheila went into the 'Home and Abroad Nursing Service'.

She had spent several difficult and traumatic years in the north of Newfoundland before deciding to work her way across Canada. Now she was working in a hospital in Toronto and had a flat of her own. I'd told her about the expected baby, asking for information about doctors and hospitals in Canada and how the system worked. Sheila told me all she knew. Then she made a generous offer. She suggested that, nearer the time of the birth, I and the boys should come and stay with her. She wrote that she had a gynaecologist and paediatrician all lined up for me.

Besides, my dental appointment was drawing near. I was still much troubled by toothache, especially at night. Sometimes on such slight threads do big decisions hang.

Ronald and I never really considered this proposal. Toronto was a long way off. It would be costly to get there and anyway, we had planned long ago, if at all possible to stick together. But it was very kind of her and it made us feel a bit more secure – a friend to call on if things went badly wrong.

Then came two letters from British Columbia. One from Ronald's sister Eileen. She was two years older than him and had come out to Canada with her husband, Harold and young daughter, Hilary several years before. Harold had got a good job in the grain business in Vancouver and was doing well. We hadn't told Eileen we were emigrating to Canada till preparations were well on the way. When she did hear she wrote us a letter, as we expected she would, saying conditions were difficult in Canada especially on farms and if we were thinking of increasing our family (she knew of my wish for a large one) it would be quite out of the question. Now, faced with the *fait accompli* her tone had completely changed. The letter was pleasant and helpful and she proposed coming to see us at Easter weekend unless they heard to the contrary. We were delighted but a little apprehensive at the suggestion. How lovely it would be to see them but what ever would they think of the shack?!!

The other letter came written in a less familiar hand and was addressed to Ronald. He opened it eagerly.

"It's from Bucky," he said.

Bucky had been a friend of his in Scotland but had come out to British Columbia several years before. We had heard he wasn't too enthusiastic about his new homeland, nor his job with the Forestry Commission. Ronald had written him a short letter letting him know of our arrival and how we had found things. We weren't sure if he would reply and we certainly didn't expect the letter Ronald now read out.

> Dear Ronald and Margaret,
> How very nice to hear from you. I write by
> return of post to offer my sincere condolences
> on your arrival in Canada, this awful country. At
> the moment you will be in a state of severe
> shock, which will change shortly to thoughts of
> suicide, and then to the certainty that you must
> get out of this bloody country at the first
> opportunity. Later one gets to the resigned stage
> beyond which only morons and lunatics pass.
> It's typical of the bloody fools – no water in the

> house and fifty yards away the most up to date
> pump in use to draw oil from the earth ...

Ronald and I couldn't help laughing. At least we didn't feel that bad about Canada – not yet anyway!

After the initial explosion in words, the letter became helpful. Perhaps he would be able to get a better job for us in BC – looking after a herd of pedigree cattle. The herd was owned by someone he knew and a modern house went with the job.

Enclosed with Bucky's letter was a short one from his wife. It said that Bucky dreamed of Scotland, night and day, but had adapted himself well to the Canadian way of life. They hoped to be able to come and see us sometime.

When Ronald came in that night and after we had tea, we talked over every aspect of Bucky's letter.

"What do you think of the job he is more or less offering us?" I asked.

Ronald hesitated. " . . . Well we chose Alberta. I really would like to give it a try. The job Bucky offers us is a thousand miles away. I don't honestly think we should move that distance yet, to something that may turn out to be a mirage. In that part of Canada there might not be many other farming jobs available."

I agreed with Ronald. In spite of our difficulties and dangers I didn't feel like moving just yet either. I felt fit enough, although sometimes very tired. Besides, my dental appointment was drawing near. I was still much troubled by toothache, especially at night. Sometimes on such slight threads do big decisions hang.

Chapter 9

The Man from the Railway

One Tuesday morning, in the week following our visit to the Jones family, I woke up wondering why it was going to be a great day. Then I remembered – I was going to the dentist. How circumstance can alter the kind of day to which one looks forward. It would be sheer heaven not to have toothache any more.

I got the children up especially early and was ready for the milk truck at 7.30. By 8.30 we were sitting outside the dentist's door. I warned the boys to be good and assured Mrs Muller that it wouldn't take long to pull the tooth.

The building where the dentist had his business was not one of Red Deer's latest. It was rather old in fact – a frame house with a flat roof badly in need of a fresh coat of paint. The surgery was on the second floor. I walked up the stairs as quickly as I could and pinged open the door marked DENTIST. At the desk sat the receptionist. She looked neat, cool and efficient.

I gave the girl my name and said, "I have an appointment at eight thirty."

"I'm sorry," she said, "the dentist's having the day off."

For a moment I was too stunned to speak and then finding my voice said,

"A day off – but I . . . I . . ."

"I'm sorry," the girl repeated without any real feeling in her voice.

"Can I make another appointment for you?"

"It will have to be a Tuesday," I said. "Next Tuesday," I ventured brightening a little.

"The dentist sure is busy just now. The first Tuesday I can offer you is in a month's time."

I explained my predicament about the bad toothache and how it kept me awake half the night but could see I was getting nowhere. I returned to the waiting truck and told Mrs Muller what had happened.

"They'd never keep you waiting that long in Scotland if you were in pain," I said.

"They do here, sometimes," she admitted with a certain resignation in her voice. "You see, this particular dentist was an inmate for several years in a concentration camp before coming here. Toothache is nothing to what he had to suffer."

I kept quiet. I had learned another lesson in relativity.

At lunch time I told Ronald all about it and then said,

"I haven't mentioned a doctor to Mrs Muller yet. Just suppose the local doctor has also been through a concentration camp and has the same attitude?"

Ronald looked worried. I hadn't meant my words, spoken partly in jest, to have that effect, so added quickly,

"Don't worry, I'm keeping well enough at the moment. Remember I've had three babies already, none of which gave much trouble apart from the kidney problem which hasn't reappeared as yet. After all I am a nurse and you an expert lamber. Babies or lambs, it's all the same really."

Ronald didn't look convinced but didn't say much.

Almost as though some outside 'other' had been listening to our problems, fate took an unexpected turn. Not long after Ronald had returned to work, Richard who happened to be looking out of the window said,

"Mummy, there's a man coming down the path."

I was at the door before he had time to knock. In front of me stood a tall thin man, his city suit showing under an open parka.

After asking my name and making sure he had come to the right house he said,

"I'm from the railway company that sponsors you folk. May I come in?" he asked politely.

I led him into the kitchen, cleared some clothes from the Winnipeg couch and asked him to sit down. The cabin was rather untidy. After returning from the dentist I hadn't felt like doing much. I'd made the lunch, the remains of which lay on the sea chest that we had used as a table ever since Bill had brought our luggage from Red Deer station. I felt the stranger looking surreptitiously round, taking everything in.

"I'm Jim Stewart," he said by way of introduction. "My company always sends someone to call on new immigrants after they have had time to settle, to see how they are making out."

Here was my chance but I must be careful and not complain too much. I'd better not mention the doctor. I didn't want to go into a discussion about my condition. Our sponsors didn't officially know about the expected baby. He must have noticed but kept discreetly quiet about it. I told him of the lack of plumbing – no tap water! He brushed this aside as nothing.

"Not many places around here have plumbed in water but it will come – it will come. They just haven't gotten around to fixing it yet."

Then I told him that the fifty dollars we got a month (about eight pounds a week) could feed us and no more. Once again he hedged.

"Well that sure is about the usual pay. New immigrants working on farms in Alberta don't get much more than that. In fact it's good. On a wheat farm you can get less and there's no work in the winter."

I told him about Ronald's long, long hours. Again he brushed this aside. He did, however, seem genuinely perturbed about the conditions in which we lived – no covering on the floor, no furniture of any kind.

"Not up to our standards at all," he said.

I handed him a cup of coffee and a biscuit and wondered what their standards were. He didn't say much more and was in a hurry to leave as soon as he had finished his coffee. He gave no promise of improvement and little hope of any immediate shift to another farm.

"Difficult at this time of year," he said. "It ain't really Spring until the end of May around here. There isn't much to do on the land until the frost begins to loosen up."

He gave me the impression of being a man without backbone. I didn't expect much action.

That evening, after the children were asleep, Ronald and I

discussed Jim Stewart's visit.

"I saw the man," said Ronald. "He parked his car outside the dairy this afternoon. He didn't speak to me, just to Shylock (Ronald's private name for his boss) who happened to be helping me for once. They disappeared into the house. I saw Muller again at milking time. He said nothing but seemed even more surly than usual. I didn't realise the man had been down to see you."

I told Ronald all that Jim Stewart had said.

"Umm," said Ronald. "Doesn't look very hopeful for any immediate action, does it?"

"No," I agreed, "but after he left, I felt a new resolve in myself. I do believe I am recovering from the shock of coming here. I feel a new confidence stirring. One of these days I *will* ask Mrs Muller about a doctor. Also I've made a decision. It's Easter at the weekend. Eileen and Harold will be here. I'm going to unpack our boxes and make the cabin look as nice as I possibly can. It depends on how you look at it certainly, but this place does have things going for it – the wonderful sunshine, the squirrel in the porch, the tap-tap-tap of the woodpeckers, the aurora borealis at night, warmth in the cabin, enough food, happy children."

Ronald had had a hectic day in the byre and was tired. He was non-committal but didn't try to stop my plans.

"Well it does look as though we'll be here until after the baby's born at least," was his only comment.

Next morning I got the children up early again, gave them breakfast, dressed them and set to work with enthusiasm.

"Boys," I said, taking them into my confidence, "I'm going to unpack our boxes today. Now if you're careful with everything, you can help."

Apart from Richard, they were more of a hindrance than a help but they did enjoy the morning. So did I. First I tackled the small room (a quarter of the cabin) adjacent to the boy's bedroom. The small red carpet we had brought was exactly the right size for the floor. We had wall-to-wall carpeting. I placed the walnut coffee table (the one piece of furniture which I couldn't find the heart to leave behind) in the centre of the room. Against the far wall I placed a row of Arthur Mee's richly bound encyclopaedia volumes. They had never looked more impressive. Then I unearthed some of our carefully packed pictures. Three of them were Japanese prints of geisha girls and gardens – a wedding present we had received five years before. Not exactly appropriate but they looked good on the wall and were light and easy to hang. When I had finished I surveyed the room. It looked good. It would look even better when I got Ronald to fix up the lamp, the one brought from home, shaped like a flame. At night it would give a warm moving glow to the room.

I looked around at my handiwork before going to prepare Ronald's lunch. No chairs – oh well – never mind; perhaps in the evening we can pretend we are Japanese kneeling on the floor and drink make-believe glasses of hot saki from the low walnut table with its beautiful markings. When Ronald came in at lunch time he was surprised and impressed at what I had been able to achieve.

In the afternoon I set to with the rest of the house. That was more difficult. I had plenty of decorative plates and ornaments but nowhere to put them. I thought they were best left locked in the chest where the children couldn't get at them. There were, however, two long glossy brown tiles, one depicting Mr Pickwick and the other Mr Snodgrass. They looked well hanging on the wall behind the cook-stove. The Shanry (the name of our farm back in Scotland) curtains made good covers for the sea-chest-table and the Winnipeg couch, hiding a lot of deficiencies. There was nothing I could do about the two smaller chests that served as benches, other than not look that far down.

Next day I got busy with scissors, needle and thread and made curtains for all the windows, cutting down some of those I had brought from home. By Good Friday we were ready for the visitors.

Chapter 10

Exploring

Eileen and Harold had told us, in their letter, that they would fly to Leduc airport, hire a car, drive to Red Deer, find a motel where they would stay the night and then be out to see us on Friday morning. Ronald had told Muller about the visit and, rather to his surprise, was given a half day off provided he worked extra hours at the weekend. The eagerly awaited visitors duly arrived just after eleven. They drew up at the top of the track in a large and shining Pontiac dwarfing our ramshackle home still further. How wonderful to see them again. It's hard to explain to those who have not been in similar circumstances, how it feels to have this kind of contact with home. It gives one a sense of wholeness again and a glowing warmth inside.

Harold and Eileen were accompanied by their daughter Hilary, now fourteen and promising to be as pretty as her mother. Harold's sister had also come with them. She was a shy and ladylike person, slim and immaculately dressed.

I wasn't quite sure when they would arrive but made a pot of soup and plenty hamburgers ready to fry.

When Harold heard that Ronald was free in the afternoon he suggested we should all go a run somewhere – see some of the world around us.

"Where would you like to go?" he asked. I had no hesitation in replying,

"Toward the Rocky Mountains."

The sleek green Pontiac took off. First it re-traced its tyre marks to Red Deer where it left Hilary and Morag to do an afternoon's shopping. Ronald sat in the front with Harold. I sat in the back with the boys, Eileen and the cine camera which took up more than its fair portion of room.

Harold consulted a map. "How about heading for a place called Rocky Mountain House," he said, "It's not too far away."

I thought this a wonderful idea. The name conjured up all sorts of pictures in my mind. Ronald agreed also.

Eileen spent most of the journey under the black cloth of the cine camera. She started to take pictures before we left Red Deer.

"She only takes pictures of the bigger buildings," Harold said with kindly laughter in his voice, "hospitals, service stations and such like. She sends film and photographs home and doesn't want to give a poor impression of Canada."

Eileen, engrossed in what she was doing, came out from under the black cloth for a moment.

"I've got a beauty of the water tower. It's quite a landmark," she said. "I've never seen a bigger one."

Once we left Red Deer there was little to see worthy of Eileen's camera until we reached Sylvan Lake. It was breathtakingly beautiful. The lake lay large and sparkling under a speedwell sky. Its surface, a mass of small white motionless waves. They must have been snap frozen as a passing wind lifted and curled the water one day in the previous autumn. Round the banks of the lake, spruce trees grew. Half hidden between their dark green ranks stood brightly painted cabins waiting for summer – hundreds of them.

But if Sylvan Lake impressed us, Rocky Mountain House certainly did not. Perhaps we were expecting too much. Harold's guide book had told us that it was the starting point for all the big game hunters, venturing into the Rocky Mountains in search of bear and moose. Once it had been one of the loneliest of trading posts on the Saskatchewan river. At that time, in the first half of last century, Alberta as a province was non- existent and the river was one of the many that ran through an enormous area known as Prince Rupert's Land. It belonged to the Hudson Bay Company and stretched for thousands of miles from the American border to the Arctic sea. I had expected some sort of township sitting at the foot of the mountains. But here the Rockies seemed a long way off. The Rocky Mountain House that we saw was a row of dusty colourless ramshackle houses enhanced only by a covering of snow. It also appeared to be deserted. I wondered if this was what they called a ghost town.

Harold drove further on. The guide book said that to the west stood an important ruin of a fort which was well worth seeing. It took longer than we thought to get there. The road became quite rough and eventually we found we were running along the edge of a precipice. When we arrived we could only wonder at what the Canadians meant by well worth seeing, because compared to our ruins in Scotland there was nothing to see – just two rough columns of stone that had once outlined a fireplace. However, it was interesting in that a placard informed us that for seventy years in the eighteenth century this had been the most northerly point in the Blackfoot Indian country, and that David Thomson (a Scotsman) had lived here with his half-breed wife. It was from this point that he set out to discover the Columbia river.

Everyone had to admit that although the fort was nothing to write home about the view was magnificent. We looked down a steep precipice into a ravine where a river wound through spruce trees. Far away the mountains were stark, rugged, beckoning. I thought of the future – one day perhaps – one day I'd get there.

We arrived back in Red Deer as it was growing dark. All things considered I don't know if we ever had a better Good Friday.

Next morning they were out at the cabin early, all set to help me. Harold chopped wood, enough to do for several days, Hilary played with the boys, Eileen helped prepare lunch while Morag hung out washing. In the frosty air, clothes on the line went as hard as boards, but if left for several days became soft and dry. Morag also offered to pump water for me. Ronald happened to see her at the pump on his way home to lunch and heard the delicate ring of her slim silver bangles chiming in the frosty air. He could hardly suppress a smile. She had obviously never done anything so rustic before and something dreadful had happened; one of her beautiful long manicured finger nails had broken off chipping her nail varnish!

While preparing lunch, Eileen and I had a chance to talk. I told her we intended moving from here at the first opportunity and that a representative from our railway sponsors had called to see us at the beginning of the week. I didn't go into any discussion as to plans for the birth of the baby. Discreetly Eileen didn't ask – nor did she, much to my relief, show any alarm at the way we were living other than to point out the hazardous state of the electric wiring and to suggest ways of lessening the danger. All her advice was helpful and practical. She told me how much she enjoyed seeing the children.

I thought how strange life was. Here we were, a gathering of Scottish people, thousands of miles from our homeland. In the middle of a huge sub-Arctic continent we were a tiny laughing island in a vast empty sea of land waves. Our small beam of light would be shining from our square window on to snow and trees. From above we would appear an insignificant star, hardly noticed, lost in the the much greater light of the aurora borealis sweeping across the snow and the leaping burning brands coming from the land. A hundred years ago, before the Province of Alberta existed, the immense expanse of Prince Rupert's land was almost devoid of people. Then only a few Indians and a handful of white men belonging to the Hudson Bay Company and calling themselves 'A Company of Adventurers', would ever pass this way. Then the animals held dominion. Hordes of North American bison roamed and grazed here when the earth became green with the short curly grass that the first settlers christened prairie wool; here the bear lived almost unmolested; the wolves and coyotes hunted under the stars as they had done for thousands and thousands of years.

On Sunday our visitors left. We were sad to see them go. Their visit was like something out of time.

"Now remember," Eileen said on leaving, "we have a basement flat. If you ever get into real difficulties you can have the flat for as long as you need it."

Harold said, "I don't know when I've enjoyed a break so much."

We could see he genuinely meant what he said. Afterwards I tried to work out why this should be. I came up with the conclusion that perhaps it was because here with us, he had touched basics. This was no weekend at the lakeside cabin with axe and matches. This was no pretending to be woodsman for a little while – this was 'for real' as the Canadians would say.

Things might have seemed tame to us after that weekend but something happened as unexpectedly as, I had been told, the warm chinook wind sometimes blows over the frozen prairie. At lunch the next day Ronald came in with the news.

"We're leaving here on Wednesday. You'll have to do the packing. I'll probably to work up to the last minute. Muller told me this morning that our sponsors had phoned to say they're shifting us to a mixed farm the day after tomorrow – somewhere east of Edmonton. That's all the information I got. Muller was not in a good mood."

Chapter 11

Again into the Unknown

Two days later, at a quarter past ten in the morning, the children and I plus some of our luggage, were unceremoniously dumped by Muller at Red Deer station. He then drove off at speed barely saying goodbye.

At that time in the morning the station was empty of people. I walked over to the ticket booth. The clerk behind the desk rattled open the hatch. I asked for tickets to Edmonton. As he handed them to me my eyes filled with tears. To my relief the ticket clerk took no notice, perhaps he was too embarrassed to say anything, perhaps he was used to women's tears and counted them of little worth. I didn't want the children to see me crying so distracted their attention by getting them to look out the waiting room window.

"Keep looking," I said, "and you'll see the train coming."

Then I sat down on the long bench and, taking out my handkerchief, repaired the damage as best I could.

Inwardly I looked for a reason for the tears. Was it because we were leaving Red Deer to travel again into the unknown? – because I was tired after the rush to get away? – because I was journeying without Ronald if only for a short time?

There must have been a real dust up between Muller and our railway sponsors because Muller had been ordered to pay our fare back to Edmonton. He couldn't take all of us in his truck, plus all the luggage, but must have thought it cheaper to take Ronald and the bulk of luggage in his Dodge while we went by train. Perhaps he had some business to do in Edmonton at the same time. He hadn't given an explanation.

By the time the train drew up at the station I had gained control and was able to make sure our luggage got on the train.

Then I helped the boys up the steps into the railroad car dragging my ungainly pregnant body after them.

Once we were all aboard and seated I felt better. The boys were excited at the prospect of travelling again.

"It's fun isn't it, travelling on trains and going to live in different places," I said, to keep my own and their spirits up. "I wonder what the new farm will be like?"

As on the journey here, which already seemed a long time ago, I looked out of the train window for houses that might be attached to farms. Again I was disappointed. On most of the farms we passed there was just one frame house which often looked rather dilapidated. Where there was a second dwelling it looked little better than the one we had just left. I gave up worrying about it – perhaps things would be better in other parts of Alberta.

On arriving at Edmonton we went for a meal in the station buffet to wait for Ronald. Afterwards the children ran around the warm enclosed station. This time I was less frightened anything would happen to them.

Ronald arrived at last. It was like the sun coming over the horizon.

"Muller took his time about leaving Redwoods," he said, "and when we got here, he stood and watched me unload all the luggage from his truck. A passing railway worker told him to help the gentleman off with his baggage. Muller was mad!" Ronald chuckled at the memory. "Well I must say I'm glad to see the back of him!"

Muller had handed Ronald, metaphorically speaking, over to the railway sponsors as though he were some unwanted property and left promptly. Ronald was instructed by them to take the afternoon train going east and disembark (again just a few miles further on!) at the township of Sandyhills, near to the border where Alberta and Saskatchewan meet. As before, the 'few miles' turned out to be much more than that and was, in fact, well over a hundred. Again our future employer would be at the station to meet us. His name was Tom Jacobs. He owned a section of land (which we now knew meant 640 acres) near to the railroad. The farm had no name, only a number.

We had another half hour to wait for the train going east. All aboard, once again, we settled down for what was to be a tedious journey. The vast expanse of land that we passed through was almost featureless. It looked cold and forbidding under a leaden sky foretelling more snow. Exhausted, I fell asleep lulled by the soporific swaying of the train. We'd been up late the night before packing. With Muller taking every last ounce of manpower possible from Ronald, he hadn't finished work in the dairy until 10.30pm. Nevertheless, in spite of the rush, everything was properly packed except for the coffee table. We just hadn't time to nail it back into its crate. I quickly made a large bag for it out of a sheet to keep it from getting scratched and hoped it would make the journey unscathed. Now with thoughts of survival uppermost in our minds the value of objects, however much prized, was diminishing.

I woke to some one shaking my shoulder.

"We're nearly there," said Ronald.

I looked out the window. The land still looked cold, white and almost featureless. It was snowing. In the distance, where the wave-like contours were straightening out into the table-flat prairies of Saskatchewan, a tall grain elevator appeared on the skyline. There was little else to attract the eye apart from a ridge of low hills showing sand in places where the dry, feather-light snow had been blown away.

Almost at the border, I mused, which sent me pondering on the one bit of information about it that I had. There were no rats in Alberta. No rats had ever crossed the border into Alberta. We'd been told this categorically. How did they know? –What stopped them? How did the Albertans keep them at bay? My mind shifted to the landscape again. There was no sense of grandeur here as there had been at Redwoods – no tall kingly spruce trees, no leaping oil flames – only emptiness and inconsequential patches of scrub birch and poplar. It was April but Spring hadn't come to this land. There was no hint of green anywhere. Back home, I thought wistfully, the daffodils will be dancing in our old orchard. Leaves will be pushing out from pale green buds and a spindrift of white blossom covering the plum trees. Fields, down in the valley, would be emerald, so green that if nature had made flames green instead of red-yellow the fields would seem on fire.

The woo-oo-ooo of the train brought me back to the present. It gradually reduced speed – the brass bell clanged loudly in the cold air – we were at Sandyhills. Our new boss, Tom Jacobs, was there to meet us – a broad-shouldered man, wearing a wide-brimmed stetson and a fur lined parka stretched over a large stomach. He was pleasant enough but this time we were reserving our judgement. He packed us all into his large car. On the way to our new home he chatted to us more than Muller had done.

I think we had given up hope of having anything special in the way of a house so we were not too disappointed or surprised when we stopped at a shack similar to the one we had just left. This one was a bit bigger, however, and more substantial to look at. Again it was made from long slats of machined wood with the bark removed. The roof was 'tiled' with wooden shingles. The shack had no porch this time. In its place was an open veranda (that we later learned to call a deck), four wide steps leading up to a platform of wood. An outer wooden door and an inner screen door led directly into the kitchen. The latter resembled the one we had just left, except that it was furnished with table and chairs and boasted a large fridge. The same black log-burning stove took up a large part of the kitchen, although it was not quite such a magnificent model as the one at Redwoods. At one end of the cabin, there was a smaller room, furnished sparsely but with two beds for the boys. The other half of the shack, facing south, looked onto a gravel road and was divided into two rooms – one furnished with a table of sorts and a few odd chairs and the

With thoughts of survival uppermost in our minds the value of objects, however much prized, was diminishing.

other almost completely filled by an enormous and substantial white enameled bed that had seen better days. The enamel was badly chipped in places and large patches of rusty iron showed through. The only other piece of furniture in the bedroom was a tall filing cabinet, rather bashed about but with four roomy drawers that slid easily out and in. The furniture certainly wasn't up to much, but compared to our last house it was luxury.

This time we had arrived in our new home before daylight had quite faded and were able to get an idea of our surroundings. The whole farm complex was arranged in much the same way as the lonely Hudson Bay forts had been in the last century. It was not, however, surrounded by a tall picket fence culminating in high gates to keep out marauding Assineboine or Blackfoot Indians as it would have been in the old days. It was open to the prairie. At the top end of a huge rectangle stood the farmhouse. A road ran past it. Our new home stood at the far end of one of the long sides close to an attractive Dutch barn. A gravel road ran past it also. At the bottom end of the rectangle low willow trees screened off a small grass paddock surrounded by a fence of wooden slats. On the side opposite to us was Mrs Jacobs' kitchen garden and a large feed lot for cattle which when writing home to mother I called a corral, thinking it sounded more romantic.

Apart from the fixtures there were a number of large implements sitting out in the open, plus three monster tractors and an enormous combine. Everything was placed neatly. Jacobs was a well-organised and tidy man. Implements rarely suffered from rust in this dry cold climate, so things left outside came to no harm. Even heaps of grain were left out over the frozen winter.

Our house sat in a slight hollow and was screened off from the rest of the yard by a large triangle of scrub trees. They were mostly birches with silver-white trunks which in letters home to my mother I called cottonwoods, thinking it made them sound different and exciting. This wood was the one untidy bit of the yard, with small implements lying here and there, plus three old iron barrels and an unusual galvanised tub which turned out to be an early washing machine with hand- operated plungers. In front of the wood sat a tall and ancient ranch wagon. At the far end of the shack, above a stretch of grass grown wild, ran a long washing line strung between two wooden poles. Near to it sat a rickety saw bench and a pile of unsawn timber. Directly across from the cabin, between Mrs Jacobs' garden and the feed lot, stood our outside toilet, a two seater of ample dimensions. Diagonally across, in the garage at the side of the farmhouse was a tap which gave us our water supply. It was a long way to go for water. It seemed especially long on the return journey when arms were nearly pulled out of sockets by the heavy weight of the full pails. It is perhaps unnecessary to mention that I learned to conserve water and that the precious fluid was used for many things before it was finally flung out.

At first, of course, we had only a cursory view of all this. Jacobs left us at the door of the shack after helping us in with our luggage. Before leaving he said,

"When you folks get sorted out come over to the house and Betty will fix a meal for you all."

I presumed Betty was his wife. Surprised at this unexpected kindness, I was perhaps over-profuse in my thanks.

Darkness had fallen by the time we climbed down the veranda steps and walked through the inch of fine fresh snow to the Jacobs' back door. Unlike our house, the farmhouse had no trees near it. It stood starkly open to the four prairie winds. It looked better at night, its shabby whiteness hidden in the darkness. A yellow glow coming from one window, lay reflected diagonally in four squares on the white ground. The house looked warm and inviting. The woman's voice too, that shouted to us to come in when we reached the door, was friendly. We entered and took our snow boots off in the small porch placing them on the pages of the Prairie Gazette laid there for that purpose. The smell of cooking beef was in the air mixed with the fine aroma of percolating coffee. Mrs Jacobs introduced herself,

"Hi you folks, nice to see you. I'm Betty Jacobs."

Mrs Jacobs was tall, slim and neatly dressed. She might have been termed pretty but for the unbecoming spectacles she wore. Her bearing was a little reserved but friendly for all that. She introduced us to their two pretty daughters, Mandy and Susan. Soon we were all crammed round her table in her new kitchen, enjoying hamburgers with apple pie and cream to follow.

The talk round the table was kept fairly general but we learned that before Betty Jacobs was married she had been the local teacher and the farmhouse had actually been the old schoolhouse where she had lived. Recently a new and larger school had been built in Sandyhills, and a new house to go with it. The Jacobs had bought the old one and brought it to the farm in sections. Our little house had also been brought, only recently, from a nearby homestead. I was astonished at all this shifting of houses. It wasn't so much take up your bed and walk as 'take up your house and travel!'

We didn't stay long after we had eaten. It had been all too much for Ronnie. He had fallen asleep at the table. We thanked the Jacobs for their hospitality and made our way back across the yard. Jacobs had put on the outside light so that we could see where we were going. We climbed up the steps of our cabin and opened the two doors. There was a wonderful warm glow coming from the fire that Ronald had banked up with logs before we left. The aroma of woodsmoke was everywhere.

"It's not such a bad old wilderness after all," Ronald said as he helped me put the boys to bed.

"No," I answered in hopeful tones. I felt the tension of the last few months slowly slipping from my shoulders.

"No it's not," I said again thoughtfully. "I expect it's too early to say for sure, but I think we've fallen among better people."

Chapter 12

Eastern Alberta & the Early Pioneers

Jacobs was a very different kind of man to Muller. Within a week of our arrival he said to Ronald, "I see your wife's expecting a baby."

The Mullers had never once mentioned the fact although it was obvious to all.

"Has she seen a doctor since coming to Canada?" Jacobs inquired, in a matter of fact manner.

"No," Ronald replied, "there's never been the opportunity."

"Well, she'll need to pay a visit to the the doctor in Sandyhills as soon as possible and he'll book her into the local hospital for the delivery. We sure have a good hospital here. It's new – one of the most up-to-date in Alberta. Betty'll make an appointment for her and take her to the surgery."

That same week Ronald tentatively told Jacobs that he would like to purchase a second hand car, saying that he could afford to do so if it wasn't too expensive.

"No problem," said Jacobs at once. "I'll take you to the best used car lot around. You sure can get cheated by some of them if you don't know what you're doing."

Jacobs seemed pleased that Ronald could afford to buy a car. We certainly would not have been able to on the pay given to us by Jacobs which was even less than we had received from Muller. Higher wages were given for work in a dairy.

With these two matters settled, the doctor and the car, we felt a good deal happier. Jacobs was true to his word and one day took Ronald to a used-car lot. They came back proudly with a big pale green Chevrolet. Its windscreen was pitted, it had seen better days but Jacobs pronounced it sound and not bad for the money. Most windscreens had a degree of pitting. Cars passing in a hurry threw up stones from the gravel ruts. It was unavoidable – apart from in Sandyhills itself no roads around here were paved, not even the major one to Edmonton.

"They haven't gotten around to it yet," Betty Jacobs told me, "except in Sandyhills itself and the reason for that is, there is an army camp on the outskirts. We sure are lucky here!"

We saw what she meant when we visited another township, months later, after heavy rain. In the small township of Pioneer we slithered and slipped madly about always fearful of sticking in a sea of mud.

The following week Betty Jacobs drove me to the doctor 's surgery. It was fortunate for us that the doctor , although born in Canada, had Scottish parents and a Scottish wife. He was a young man and like many Scots, not given to wasting words. He examined me, pronounced me fit and made another appointment for me in a month's time. He said he would book me into the local hospital. I suggested having the baby at home.

"In Scotland mothers have their babies at home if they want to," I told him.

He seemed rather shocked at the idea and said it just wasn't done in Alberta. In fact it was against the law. I left it at that. It wasn't until a long time afterwards that we realised how fortunate we were to fall into the hands of that particular doctor. There were charlatans in the medical profession just as there were in car sales.

Betty Jacobs had been so kind I decided not to mention dentists just yet. Besides, my errant tooth had got a bit bored aching and had settled down a bit.

Ronald and I decided things were definitely looking up. True there were things I missed about Redwoods. The landscape was really barren here. There were no stately trees, no drumming woodpeckers, no friendly squirrel to greet us in the morning – nothing except the ominous croak of the raven and the howling at night of the ubiquitous coyote. Winter was still hard on the land and showed little sign of letting up.

Jacobs had about two hundred cattle in his feed lot. He kept them to use up the surplus grain that nobody wanted. The boom years in grain were gone. To begin with Ronald spent much of his working day among the cattle as well as doing all sorts of odd jobs. Occasionally there wasn't much to do at all, but Jacobs never liked to waste a second of his hired man's time. Once Ronald was sent to make holes for posts – an almost impossible task in winter for the uninitiated.

"It's like chipping away at concrete," he told me afterwards. "It's frozen, virgin soil where, even in the summer, you don't need to go far down before you reach permafrost Jacobs told me!"

It was those kind of discoveries that brought home to us how new this land was to any form of cultivation.

The first white settlers who had come to people the Westlands had arrived only in the last century. The first settlement began a good way east of Sandyhills, below Lake Winnipeg on the banks of the Red River. It was the brain child of Lord Selkirk from Kirkcudbrightshire in Scotland, one of the heads of the Hudson Bay Company. He brought over some of his own countrymen and women, whole families in fact, directing them to where he knew the virgin soil was good. Many of the families who volunteered to come were from the Highlands and Islands. Landlords had given crofters notice to leave in order to make more room for sheep at a time when the latter were a profitable enterprise. If the crofters didn't go quietly they set fire to the thatched roofs of their stone-built cottages. It may have been easy to persuade these displaced persons with nowhere to go to take the plunge and emigrate to another country.

I wondered if they had any idea of the rigours and hardships that lay before them. Had they been told the whole truth, I doubt if many would have attempted it. What must have been their thoughts when, after a long and arduous sea voyage, they arrived on the desolate shores of the Hudson Bay – men, women and children – to find that their journey was only beginning! They had yet to cross a vast uninhabited terrain. They travelled mainly down river by canoe, oared by Swampy Cree Indians. From time to time, when they came to rapids or impassable water, the canoes had to be taken out of the river and carried along the wild overgrown tracks hewn out by a few fur traders on their way south to Fort Garry. Also at places where the water was too shallow, the passengers had to disembark and the canoes were pulled along empty. Sometimes these portages, as they were called, went on for miles and miles. It was often tough going, wading up to their waist in muddy ooze, through muskeg or making their way over uncleared bushland, thick with scrub trees, the ground littered with fallen branches. Always they were in danger of attack from an angry bear. Occasionally a moose would cross their path or a wolf. Through the trees they might catch glimpses of shy martins or the swift cat-like lynx. When the opportunity arose they would try to shoot something for the pot to vary their meagre diet based largely on pemmican, an Indian preparation of buffalo meat. If they were lucky they might bag a duck, goose or more rarely, a moose. Also they would doubtless find wild cranberries or saskatoons having that sharp sweet taste of the tundra.

On top of everything else they would have to endure a variety of biting insects – clouds of them, all waiting to inject or suck the immigrants' fresh sweet blood – mosquitos and flies, from the ferocious 'bulldogs' (bluebottle size) to the almost microscopic insects that the Indians called no-see-ums which gave a far nastier bite than any midge from the glens or hillsides of Scotland.

How eerie it must have been at night as they lay awake listening to the noises of these strange wild places, the grunt of a bear, howl of a wolf, crazy laugh of a loon across the water at sundown. They were probably people well-versed in the bible. I wondered if they saw themselves as a tribe being led through the wilderness to some land of Goshen. If so they must have got a shock when they saw their Goshen because there was nothing – nothing there at all. They had to start from scratch and clear the land. If we grumbled about no furniture, they had no house and would have to build one, were it only a sod hut, before early winter set in with its searing frosts.

In some respects Selkirk was a poor Moses, letting his people fend for themselves, having made no proper provision for them. They were set down among unfriendly Indians to manage as best they could. The Assineboines, angry at the white man's intrusion into their land and his destruction of their livelihood, the buffalo, were known for their murderous and scalp-hunting ways. There was no one sent to protect this little band of Scots.

It is a strange and touching story that for these first settlers there were times of such dire need that they had to go to the Assineboines for help. Sometimes these Indians, renowned for their cruelty, were gentle and kind, helping them in their distress. The miracle is that, one way or another, the little colony survived and began to cultivate the land to find that crops grew tall and yielded well.

Later on Selkirk was accused of using the settlers to prevent the Hudson Bay's rivals in fur trading, the North West Company, from getting their boats further up the river. The rival company was older than theirs and largely run by French Canadians. The line, Selkirk hoped, running up the river from Montreal to Athabasca would be cut at the point where the settlers lived.

Eventually a bigger-than-usual skirmish broke out between the rival companies, both using Indians to augment their forces and the colonists became embroiled in a fight not of their own making.

This incident, however, led to the temporary evacuation of the people of the Red River settlement to a more civilised area. Also it brought the Canadian and British governments together, both insisting that the rival fur companies unite and thereby make possible the permanent and peaceful establishment of the Red River Settlement.

Slowly more people came and began to drift further west into this land that could grow good crops, till eventually it was cleared of the huge herds of wild bison (the staple diet of the nomad Indians).

By the time we came to Alberta, all that was left of these powerful animals was a small herd kept, for their protection, on the shores of Cooking Lake, near Edmonton.

Chapter 13

The Farm near Sandyhills

In the Spring of 1959, Tom Jacobs was impatiently waiting for the frost to lift, ready to start seeding the moment it was possible. I took a photo of Ronald on his first time out on the tractor, in his fur-hooded parka and with a three cornered scarf tied across his face – muffled up against the cold – only his eyes showing.

Betty Jacobs kept up the kindness shown to us on our arrival, always coming over to see if there was anything we required. She never stayed long to chat, however, and I didn't learn as much as I would have liked about what was, for us, a new part of the world. Certainly when I asked direct questions she always answered but never enlarged on the subject and never offered any information other than what was immediately relevant to the moment.

"These small lakes," I asked one day, "that we see not far from here, they look inviting with their white sands, do you visit them when the weather is warm enough?"

"These lakes are good for nothing," she told me. "It isn't white sand that you see it's an alkali deposit."

"The road running past your house going north – where does it go to?"

Betty Jacobs thought for a moment. She looked a little taken aback as though no one had asked her that question before and she hadn't thought to question herself.

"I dunno," she said. "I guess it must go somewhere."

I thought this strange. It surprised me also that she was not in the least curious as to where we had come from or why. Anything to do with our former life held no interest for her. That we were here now to help them and that we were people in need of help ourselves were the things that mattered and she helped us gladly in a natural and unassuming manner.

Tom Jacobs was helpful too in his own way. He had diffi-culty, I think, communicating with adults, especially our sort from a different country and culture but when it came to children he had no difficulties at all. He liked children and could speak their language. The boys held him in high esteem. One day he presented them with two tricycles that his daughters had recently given up now they had bikes. Also, he showed them the way to a large sandpit where, in the long summer days that lay ahead, they were to have endless hours of fun. He let them play among old implements where everything was made as safe as possible. From time to time he would lift them up onto the high seats of the monster tractors where they felt very important indeed. He was tolerant and good humoured with the boys and Tom Jacob's place had everything a growing boy needs and with minimum restrictions.

Slowly Alberta began to seep into my blood, to become part of me, and I knew I was not rejecting this land.

I took pleasure, believe it or not, in washing. Our clothes had got rather grubby at Red-woods. Here I made full use of my galvanised tub, setting it on the hot stove each morning and boiling all the clothes that would boil. Every day I hung them out on the line to dry under a faultless prairie sky. Boiling water, frost and sun made everything satisfyingly bright and clean. I would take the clothes in at sunset, enjoying the excuse to watch this magnificent event. Golds and crimsons ever merged and moved in the wide prairie sky to fill the west with an ecstasy of colour which reflected on everything below. Sunrises were similar. If there was nothing else beautiful in this barren land, for this experience alone it was worth having come here! I never tired of looking.

Slowly Alberta began to seep into my blood, to become part

of me, and I knew I was not rejecting this land. I was learning new dimensions. In some ways 'Jacobs' Place' wasn't lonely at all. Redwoods had been lonelier, more cut off from civilisation. Here a gravel road ran past the front of our house. An occasional car passed, splaying out small stones that sometimes rattled on the cabin windows.

When the last vestiges of snow and frost had left the surface of the land, cars stirred up great clouds of dust that hung in the air like grey voile curtains long after they had gone. About two miles away and easily seen from our house, rose a large green corrugated iron shed – the local 'sell-everything' store. It would have been simple to walk there had I not had the children. It was difficult to push a pram along a gravel road. I could have driven there after we got the Chevrolet but I required a Canadian licence.

"Wait till after the baby's born," Ronald said.

Beyond the road running past the house, a couple of hundred yards further on, the super continental trains trundled their heavy way across the plains. There was a railroad crossing quite near to us. Before reaching it, each train would blow its loud whistle. The boys loved to watch these long trains, both freight and passenger, and spent a lot of time looking out the window to see if one was coming. One day Richard said in a matter of fact way,

"Mummy, all the trains whistle for me to come out and see them."

Everytime he heard the whistle, no matter what he was doing, he would rush out of the house to wave and wait till the long monster had passed.

There was a moment (Tom Jacobs knew it well) when the ground lost just enough frost on the top layers for the seed to be scattered. No ploughing was needed on this land. The surface of it was worked with discs and harrows and the seed sown.

"They don't use a plough here anymore," Ronald informed me, "they found it was causing erosion and that they didn't really need to use it anyway. It's a completely different method of farming to that back home."

It was too, and it now meant very long hours for Ronald.

Before seeding time his hours were 7am to 7pm with half a day off on Saturday and only the essential chores to do on Sunday. Now it was literally day and night. Tom Jacobs had four quarter sections of arable ground – 1,000 acres in all to be sown and three weeks or less to do it in.

"It wouldn't be so bad," Ronald complained to me one evening, "if Jacobs' quarter sections were all together but some of them are miles apart. The sensible thing to do would be for Jacobs and his neighbours to get together and re-arrange things a bit. The land looks all pretty much the same to me. Farms have not been long in existence here. The farmers don't seem to have a sense of pride or ownership about their places. Tom Jacobs told me it's just somewhere to scrape a living or make money if they're lucky and have what it takes. They do it for as long as their health lasts and then pack up and go into the city or get a cushy job in a gas station. I'll say one thing for them though, if they demand a lot from other people, they are equally hard on themselves."

Tom Jacobs never gave Ronald much more information about anything other than what he wanted him to do. Before May it looked as though the seeding of a thousand acres would have to be done by Ronald and Jacobs between them. Then one day, from across the lonely prairie, Adrian arrived.

Adrian, as the romantic novelists would put it, was tall, dark and handsome. He was English and came from the county of Somerset. He and his friend Kenneth had come to Canada the year before and had found work on a farm in Ontario. Wanting to explore fresh fields, they decided to move west. Adrian came into our lives like a chinook after hard weather. He was the laughing and irresponsible wind – didn't know the meaning of the word serious. Ronald, with all of us to care for, found it difficult not to worry, but there were no lines of worry on Adrian's young face. He could take Tom Jacobs and his tantrums very much less seriously than we could.

We had been right to reserve our judgement about Tom Jacobs on that first day at the station. He was, as we had reckoned, a fair and just man, also practical and able, but we never quite understood him. Firstly you couldn't tell him anything.

Once when a cattle beast was ill and like to die in the feed lot, Ronald ventured to tell Jacobs what he thought was wrong with it. He also told him what he thought the remedy was, as we once had similar trouble with a cattle beast back home. Jacobs didn't want to know – to the extent that he did nothing about it and the beast died. After that Ronald was taken off the feed lot altogether. He knew too much about cattle. Later, we heard he was the same with the neighbours – nobody could tell Jacobs anything. Consequently he made some terrible mistakes by which, I expect, he learned.

Secondly, he was always in a hurry. Often, in spite of his weight, we would see him running. At seven in the morning the door of the farmhouse would go bang and out would come Jacobs at the trot, holding on to his stomach as he went, making for the barn, perhaps only to scrape some rust from an implement and there was next to no rust in Alberta.

Thirdly, he was a man of dangerous moods that were difficult to assess, sometimes taking tantrums and getting in to a rage for no apparent reason. Local people wouldn't work with him because of this. To Adrian it was like water off a duck's back. He could and did take fantastic liberties with his boss that Ronald would not have dared to do, and got away with it. He would kid Jacobs about it afterwards until he won from him first a crinkle under the eyes and then a huge belly laugh.

Once, during seeding time, when Jacobs had been driving Ronald and Adrian very hard, Adrian, while working on his own in the far away field, decided to have an afternoon nap lying in the shade of his tractor. He was fast asleep when the first stone hit him. He opened a startled eye to see Jacobs raging towards him. He rose with speed, jumped on his tractor and was off across the Prairie, stones following him as he went. Later that evening he ragged Jacobs about 'the flinging of the rocks' and said how funny it must have looked! Jacobs, the heat of the moment gone, saw the funny side.

Ronald just couldn't be like that with Jacobs. For us life was too serious, although after the coming of Adrian the edge was taken off that. We were beginning to discover that although we spoke the same language as the Canadians, we didn't always have the same understanding. With Adrian it was different; being British and in similar circumstances we understood one another.

Adrian made a difference to our lives. On the days that they were not working overtime, Adrian, who lived in with the Jacobs, would saunter over to our shack after supper. Ronald and he would go over the day's happenings, Jacobs' idiosyncrasies and the alleged madness of life in Canada compared with home. Had anyone been passing on the gravel road beyond the low picket fence which ran round or small uncultivated garden, they would have heard much laughter. They would also have heard the sound of happy children's voices for Adrian used to play with them if he wasn't too tired. They loved this big new uncle that could so quickly become a boy again.

The difficulties of seeding time rubbed off on me. Ronald, as a rule, had few spare moments for anything other than work. He was often very tired. I tried to save him as much as I could. Logs had to be sawn for the fire with a blunt old saw on the makeshift saw bench; also water had to be carried – I tried to get all this done before Ronald came in for his meals. I was feeling well now, and happy getting my little house ship-shape. Betty Jacobs seemed pleased at my efforts and remarked, among other things, on the sparkling windows – she had never seen them so bright, she said. From time to time she brought things over for the house to make the cabin a little nicer – a new piece of oil cloth for the table, a rug for the floor, a vase she no longer wanted. One day she looked in and said,

"Say, you folk's kitchen sure could do with brightening up a little. How would you like some paint for the walls?"

I looked at the unpainted hardboard walls and agreed with Betty

"That would be very kind of you," I said.

"I'll bring it over right now," she said, "as long as I remember, but don't start painting till after seeding time and the baby is born. Ronald can help you with it after work."

Minutes later she brought the paint over, left it and ran off. I looked with pleasure at the pots of paint – four of them, containing clear colours, each one different, white, blue, yellow, green. The brushes too were there, clean and inviting. The children were quiet for once, playing a game in the bedroom which, with luck, would absorb them for some time. Now or never, I thought and started painting.

I got a surprising amount done that morning, and what a difference it made. The sun seemed twice as bright, dancing on the newly painted walls.

Three days later Betty Jacobs returned and saw, to her astonishment, the kitchen walls painted and me standing, rather precariously, on top of a rickety table, putting the finishing touches to the ceiling.

"Oh you shouldn't be doing that!" she said in a startled voice. "You shouldn't be reaching like that with the baby so nearly due."

I laughed and assured her I was all right as I applied the last stroke and clumsily climbed down from the table.

"You have done well," she said. "What a difference. How pretty and bright it looks." Her eyes danced with the same pleasure as mine. Did I detect a hint of admiration in them? Something I knew would be hard to come by in this difficult land. It was a good moment.

Then one day hats were thrown in the air – seeding was over – the baby was due. It had waited, thank goodness, no early delivery! It was a most accommodating baby no matter what the sex. Next day Tom Jacobs said to Ronald,

"How are you going to manage when you wife goes into hospital?"

"I don't quite know," Ronald replied. Jacobs made all the decisions about everything and Ronald knew he would come up with something so wasn't too worried.

"Perhaps I could get a woman from Sandyhills to come and look after the children while Margaret is away," Ronald continued.

"I don't think you will be able to get anyone," said Jacobs and then matter-of-factly, "You can stay off work yourself and look after them if you like."

This is just what we hoped he would say. I dreaded the thought of having to take the boys to some woman in Sandyhills whom neither I nor the children knew. Ronald was pleased also.

The next Sunday and I felt the first intimations of birth. Gentle at first and then more insistent. The doctor had asked me to get into hospital as soon as I was sure the baby was on the way. We all bundled into the car and flew along the gravel road.

"Not so fast!" I said, "there's no real hurry and after three confinements you shouldn't be nervous!"

"I'm not," said Ronald nonchalantly, "not this time."

We were now on the outskirts of Sandyhills. A car was swaying towards us, directly in our path.

"Then why are you driving on the wrong side of the road?" I asked as Ronald, with a screech of brakes shuddered over into the opposite ruts and I curled up in pain as a new and more severe contraction took me by surprise.

Chapter 14

Sugar and Spice

Wandering Siberian wastes,
Lost in a foreign land,
I look for familiars to cling to;
The same fireball hanging in outer space
That lights my native moor reaches me here
The child conceived at home
Leaps in its small dark hollow.

It wasn't until I waved goodbye to Ronald and the family from
the window of the hospital waiting room that I felt really alone
for the first time since coming to Canada. Children weren't
encouraged into the maternity department and, as there was
no one we could leave them with, Ronald had to go also. Just
what was I doing here, thousands of miles from the land of my
birth, walking along the antiseptic corridors of a foreign hospital
accompanied by a nurse who spoke a foreign English?

The maternity department had a wing all to itself. The lift
that took us up to it ran as smoothly as silk. This new hospital
was unspectacular to look at from the outside although it was
three storeys high, but inside it was bright, clean and shining, all
tiles and bright paint. I had the offer of a wheelchair to take me
to my ward but I was feeling fine now and declined. As I walked
along I got glimpses through swinging doors of theatres,
consulting rooms, plaster rooms, all glinting of steel from basins,
trolleys and instruments and into pleasantly curtained wards.
Nurses bustled past, neat in white uniforms, and doctors walked
in and out of doors with stethoscopes hanging around open-
neck shirts. They were altogether more casually dressed than
they would have been at home in the late fifties.

Before undressing in the ward I was ushered into, I walked

over to the wide window and looked out. A sense of unreality swept over me. I gave myself a pinch in order to make sure I wasn't dreaming. Beyond the window lay not the ancient Scottish town of Perth, where the three boys had been born, with its beautiful old trees, church spires, substantial stone houses rising against a backdrop of hills and a broad silver river, but an entirely new and different place. Sandyhills had sprung up comparatively recently, from a lonely, almost featureless plain and was completely alien to anything I had ever known. Built on the grid system it had one broad main street, unimaginatively called Main Street, and other roads running off it at regular right-angled intervals.

The brand new hospital had been erected at the far end of Main Street. At the back was a large expanse of ground for gardens (which hadn't materialised yet) and car parks but the front was built directly adjacent to the sidewalk. Main Street was very broad, as is usual in countries where there is no shortage of land, but the buildings which ran along it on either side, looked as if they had all just happened as necessity dictated. Most had flat roofs and were constructed of weatherboard. Some were single storey, some double as the hotel opposite, an uninspiring building used more as a rooming house than a hotel. The emporium for clothes, the liquor store, the drug store, hamburger house, the bank, were all square or elongated boxes. The beer parlour and barber's shop had low slatted wooden doors that would swing either way in order to be able to push out drunken cowboys or soldiers. On the far side of the hotel stood the untidy gas station with its tin signs that swung and creaked in the light wind and the used car lot where Ronald had got his car. There was not the slightest hint of elegance here as there was in Red Deer with its green glass dome for a water tower and its rich Peacock Restaurant, nor could you imagine it ever coming.

There were very few trees and those that did risk raising branches to the enormous sky were as yet, small and spindly. A fine dust hung in the air raised by the few cars that passed. Below my high window a solitary figure strode purposefully by, wearing tight jeans that accentuated bandy legs, a fringed frontier jacket above a tartan, open-necked shirt and a wide-brimmed stetson.

101

His hair, hanging well below his stetson, was dark and greasy, his skin swarthy. There was no spare flesh about him. I guessed him to be a cowboy down from the north looking for summer work. He had left his horse tied to a lamp post and was making for the barber's saloon on the other side of the street next to the hotel.

Here, in this small cow town, everything looked very temporary. A June sun poured in brightening the room. At least that was the same.

I undressed and put on the plain white nightgown which the nurse had given me and climbed into bed. I had not long to wait. The nurse returned accompanied by the doctor . He seemed pleased to see me. He was slim and handsome in an unassuming way with the reticence of a Scot that held an assurance for me as strong as my native hills. Bred from people belonging to a land he had never seen, he was probably quite unaware of how typical he seemed and, in my eyes, how trustworthy.

After examination he said, "The baby is on the way but there is nothing very imminent. You might have to wait some time."

Secretly I hoped not and chose to remember the sudden and unexpected arrival of my last baby. The doctor, however, was right in his prediction. It was an on and off affair – the pains starting and then petering out into frustrating times of plain waiting. Not the straight through roaring challenge I had hoped it would be. Last time the pains came in great mountain peaks that demanded to be climbed before descending into lotus valleys. Eventually after Everest heights had been reached, came the calmer waves of giving birth. Unfortunately it was never like that – never predictable. I was displaced – couldn't get into the rhythm. I had plenty of time to reminisce on other births in another land. Plenty time to go over, in my mind, the hills of home where I had learned so much about birth from sheep on the morning slopes, fresh with April; from the out-wintering Highland cattle giving birth under the trees, their calves falling onto decades of pine needles.

Twenty hours after setting foot in hospital there was still no baby and I was beginning to feel very tired. The ward I was in was pleasant. Up until now I had been its only inmate and then another mother-to-be was admitted. Eve looked very young – it was her first baby that was expected.

I had been told that when the actual birth was close, I would be shifted into the 'labour room'. I didn't like the sound of this, I wanted to be left alone not moved around. At home I had always been allowed to remain in the same bed. I enquired further and was informed by the nurse that the shift was left to the last moment because there was only one bed in the labour room and it was a case of first come first served. I also found out, after further questioning, that I would be strapped on to the bed. When the doctor came in on one of his quick visits, I asked if it was absolutely necessary to be shifted and strapped to the bed in the labour room. He looked down at me kindly and smiled, "I'm pretty well in charge here," he said. "It's not usual, but since you especially request it, we will leave you unfettered but you'll have to move through to the labour room, I'm afraid."

"And please doctor," I said as he was about to leave the room, "no anaesthetic." I had also learned from the nurse, that it was usual practice to give a whiff of anaesthetic prior to the birth.

The doctor looked a little surprised that I should want to go through the 'agonies' of childbirth unaided. At an earlier date, when visiting his surgery, I had surprised him even more. The question of his fee came up.

"How much will it cost?" I had asked.

"How much will it cost?" I had asked the doctor. "My fee is seventy dollars for a girl, eighty dollars for a boy." I was taken aback. "Eighty dollars for a boy includes circumcision."

103

"My fee is seventy dollars for a girl, eighty dollars for a boy." I was taken aback. Several ideas shifted around in my head as to why one should cost more than the other.

"Why the difference?" I asked.

"Eighty dollars for a boy includes circumcision."

"But if it's a boy I don't want him circumcised."

It was the doctor's turn to look surprised.

After he left, Eve and I lay side by side, the curtains drawn between us. We didn't speak. I suspected she was as near to giving birth as I was myself, perhaps nearer – would we both land at once, would there be one mad rush for the bed in the labour room? This thought gave me something to worry about.

At last the doctor decided my time had come and I was trundled along the passage on a trolley and helped on to the waiting labour room bed. Even here, the baby was slow but eventually the great moment arrived and I heard that first wonderful cry that sends love into immediate action.

"A girl," the doctor said triumphantly (he knew I had already three boys) and very soon he laid my naked child against my half bared shoulder – what a moment! I looked at my little seventy dollars worth – the most beautiful baby girl one could imagine!

I looked up at the doctor to thank him for his help and noticed his eyes were shining with that special love seen in the eyes of both doctors and nurses after the triumph of helping to bring another being safely into the world.

I felt tired after the birth but not sleepy. When everything was done, the doctor gone and the new born baby bathed and dressed in a long white gown, I asked what time it was.

"One o'clock in the morning," said the nurse."

How would I ever be able to wait till the following afternoon before Ronald would see his first born daughter? Normally he would have been there right after the birth to see our child. I felt cut off. I kept thinking, he won't know we have a little girl. What a lovely surprise it will be for him. It made me all warm inside to imagine the morning and Betty Jacobs rushing over to our shack with the glad tidings. I knew she also was excited by the impending birth but I couldn't disturb her at one in the morning.

"As soon as it's daylight," I asked the nurse, "could you please phone the farm and let my husband know we have a daughter?" She beamed broadly and promised she would.

I was taken back on a trolley just as Eve was brought in to the labour room. The doctor was having a busy night. I was given a pill to help me sleep which I did fitfully waking up when Eve returned to keep me company.

"What did you get?" I asked sleepily.

"Same as you," she said, "a little girl." I looked over to where Eve's long blonde hair sprawled on the pillow and saw the same look of love and release in her eyes that I knew must be in mine.

The nurse dimmed the light and left us. She took Eve's baby to join mine in the nursery in order to give us a rest, promising to bring them back at first light. Two utterly contented women, complete strangers, brought together by circumstance, knew a closeness stemming from shared experience and slept.

Just as she said she would, the nurse came in early with the babies. Oh the thrill and anxiety to a mother of that special baby cry!

"They've both been good," the nurse told us, "but now they are very hungry."

I looked at my little girl almost in disbelief. I had almost begun to take it for granted that I could produce only boys! Feeding her was no problem for me. I had breast fed the others, I could breast feed this one also. Eve wasn't so sure about breast feeding her baby. I encouraged her as best I could, but knew, from experience, that the thought was abhorrent to some sensitive souls, especially those who had been given wrong impressions when young. Their secret wish was to have the baby bottle fed although they attempted to breast feed through a sense of duty.

The morning passed pleasantly. When I wasn't nursing my child I kept looking at her sleeping in the cot and wishing it was afternoon and visiting time. Eventually it came. Ronald looked at his new child with a special soft look and the boys, although very excited, seemed a little in awe of this *rara avis* – a sister!

"Betty Jacobs came over to the house and told me first thing in the morning," Ronald said. " She was just as excited as your mother will be. She's coming to see you as soon as she's allowed in."

"How very kind of her," I said.

Betty Jacobs came to see me and the new baby next day.

"Normally this hospital will only let the husband and mother visit," she told me, "but I asked, as a special favour, to get in, explaining that your mother was far away and that you had no relatives near."

It was a happy visit. It was obvious that Betty Jacobs loved babies and I felt at home with her. Ronald and the boys came every day without fail. The boys were allowed in as we had no one we could leave them with. Ronald had Eve and me in fits of laughter, describing the details of his inept housekeeping.

Eve and I got on well together. I learned a lot from her. It was so nice, once more, to have a woman companion to chat to. Of course, we had a lot in common, even although our backgrounds were completely different. Women all over the world have strong common bonds.

The doctor was always popping in to see how we were. He didn't linger long or say much. It was usual, I learned, to remain in hospital for a week after the birth of a baby. This, in Eve's case was no problem. For her, the hospital was free. But in our case we knew we would have to pay the hospital over and above the doctor 's fee. He had made enquiries and was horrified at how much actually being in hospital did cost in Alberta. He never asked us if we could afford to pay or not, but I think assumed that we would not be able to. Trying to make things possible for us he informed me that I could get home on the fourth day after the birth. I made no protest as above all, I wanted to get home. Nevertheless the doctor didn't seem happy about the situation.

"I don't like it," he said, "you were pretty exhausted after the birth and you will be going back to what are bound to be unhygienic conditions – no running water – no inside toilet – no plumbing."

Seeing no bogies, I said nothing but tried to assure him I would be all right. I got the impression he wasn't listening to me, he seemed more to be having a dialogue with himself.

On the evening before I was due to go home, the doctor entered the ward and stood at the bottom of my bed grinning broadly.

"Well I've done it!" he said, "pulled it off." He looked pleased with himself.

"Done what?" I asked

"I rang up the government offices in Edmonton, got in touch with the authorities and have got Alberta to change its laws for you."

"Change its laws for me!" I was mystified. At home it took at least two years to change laws for anyone. What law did he mean? He was talking in riddles! I looked at him questioningly.

"You remember I told you some time ago, that you required to be in Alberta for nine months before being eligible for free hospitalization? You don't now. The new law will state that if you are an authentic immigrant coming from another country, you are entitled to free hospitalization from the time you arrive. Kind of Alberta to change its laws for you, isn't it?"

I thought it little short of miraculous and felt it would be most ungracious of me to tell him I really didn't want to remain in hospital. Instead I thanked him kindly for the trouble he had taken and for his thoughtfulness. I was touched by it. He wasn't the sort of man that sought praise and made a hasty exit.

Chapter 15

Bluebirds and Brown-eyed-Susans

Spring and summer had joined hands in the week I was in hospital. The triangle of trees in front of the cabin, our own miniature forest, had come fully into leaf. Fresh and green now the branches, springing from the spindly silver-white trunks, proclaimed new life as promised.

Our patch of trees, this morsel of virgin forest, once belonged to an on-going process. If the parent trees died, new shoots flourished and grew into parent trees, or so it was until man from across the ocean came and tore them out, clearing the land to make way for wheat. Not that he could be blamed for that, but why destroy so many? It was almost as though he hated them! Too late, they discovered erosion. In some parts of Canada trees were being replanted but not here – not yet at least!

We were fortunate to have trees as there were very few about. Perhaps that is why our little bit of prairie was so well populated with birds and animals.

The birds had little in the way of song but were as bright as jewels. Cedar waxwings danced among the sunlit twigs, each varnished feather kept immaculately in place by preening, each waxed crest proclaiming some sort of kingship among the birds. Later in the season, one pair were to give us much pleasure when they taught their exquisite brood to fly close to the cabin. Humans for them, as yet, held no threat.

More modestly, small slender birds, as yellow as the tassels on the laburnum trees back home, crept among the branches. Betty Jacobs called them canaries.

The most spectacular of all the birds, however, were the bluebirds. When Ronald and I first saw one we could hardly believe it was real. It was almost as though a piece of deep blue sky had taken the shape of a bird and was sweeping towards us. Later I learned from a Canadian bird book that there are different varieties. Those that are blue all over are called Mountain Bluebirds.

The undergrowth too was busy, rustling with different kinds of squirrels. Chipmunks ran in and out of the dead wood that lay beside the saw bench. They were dainty creatures, prettier than their larger cousins. They had bushy squirrel tails, dark grey stripes on lighter grey fur, bright eyes and appealing faces.

Beyond the willows, out on the prairie proper, lay the domain of the coyotes and the gophers. The latter were squirrel-like rodents, lacking the bushy tail. They made their nest in a hole in the ground but they were always popping their heads out to have a look or standing straight up on their hind legs beside their holes to see what was happening above ground. I didn't see much of them but Ronald often saw them when he was out cultivating the land. They were no friends of the farmers, however, taking much the same role as the rabbits do back home.

Later on in the summer large and colourful butterflies fluttered about the wide yard and our little wood. There were also less pleasant visitors, namely flies, mosquitoes and wasps.

On the first day of summer, Ronald came to fetch me and our baby daughter from the hospital. The boys, in the back seat of the car, bounced with excitement at the prospect of getting us home. This time Ronald drove on the correct side of the road, making no mistakes. As we reached the trees in front of the cabin, a bluebird dipped to greet us. We made our way up the path between the cottonwoods. Ronald carried his daughter and the boys jumped ahead shouting,

"Come and see, Mummy, come and see."

I wondered what to expect. How had they really coped? Would the cabin be in a mess? The boys couldn't wait for me to climb the wooden steps and squeak open the screen door. The new paint shone on the kitchen walls, everything was tidy. The kettle sang on the cook-stove, logs were piled neatly beside it and the table was set for lunch.

"Look at the new cloth, Mummy," said Richard. "Mrs Jacobs gave it to us – isn't it nice?" and before I could get a word in edgeways continued, "I brought in all these logs, aren't there a lot?"

"I swept the floor, isn't it clean?" piped up Michael.

"The table, look the table. I put down the knives, forks, spoons," babbled Ronnie not to be outdone. They all clamoured at once. My surprise was genuine. I praised them all.

"I'm a big boy now," the precocious Ronnie continued, "come and see my new bed."

I followed him into the boy's bedroom. In between the two beds that were there before, Ronald had put a makeshift affair fashioned from one of our packing cases and supporting a mattress donated by Betty Jacobs. Ronnie seemed as pleased with it as if it had been the most expensive bed we could have bought him. It looked very safe. The way in which Ronald had squeezed it between the others ensured that Ronnie could not fall out.

Next, we trooped to the sitting room. Ronald had laid the red carpet and a vase of saskatoon blossom glowed from the window ledge. Momentarily I thought how well the round walnut coffee table would have looked in the middle of the room but sadly it hadn't withstood the journey east, arriving still sewn into the sheet, but severed down the middle.

In our room, the big brass bed was neatly made with fresh linen. Beside it Ronald had placed Ronnie's pram, now to serve as a cot for Mahri-Louise. Opposite the antediluvian bed, the scratched old filing cabinet which we used as a chest of drawers, was newly painted white and on top of it stood a number of my favourite family photographs which Ronald must have dug out from the bottom of the biggest kist. Ronald, who had followed us into the bedroom, placed Mahri-Louise carefully into her new bed.

"Oh Ronald!" was all I could say.

"I wanted to make it as homely as possible, he answered, putting his arms round my shoulders and giving me a kiss.

"Welcome home darling."

A few silent happy tears trickled down my cheeks.

"It doesn't matter where we are, does it?" I said, "as long as we are all together." I looked down at our new daughter. Already she had fallen asleep. She had been a contented baby from the beginning.

"Thank you for having such a tidy house to come back to." I turned to him.

"Don't mention it," he said modestly. "Thank the boys who were such a help and thank Adrian also. He came in last night and was determined to scrub the house from top to bottom."

How very kind people are, I thought. Somehow this was everyone's baby – everyone had helped.

Lunch was nearly over when we heard a gentle tap at the screen door and a voice saying, "May I come in?" It was Betty Jacobs.

Instinctively I knew she wanted to see the baby and I, being so lately the mother, wanted more than anything else to show her off. I wheeled Mahri-Louise through from the bedroom. She had just wakened up. I lifted her out of the pram putting her into the waiting arms of Betty Jacobs who lovingly cradled her.

"She sure has changed in those four days and my, isn't she a pretty little girl. You sure wouldn't mistake her for a boy." She held her for some time before handing her back and then told me the other reason for her visit.

"I'm giving tea this afternoon to the girls from Sandyhills W.A. Would you like to come, bringing the baby with you, of course?"

My reply was without hesitation. I wouldn't, for the world, have refused and risked hurting her feelings. She had been so kind to us. Also, always at the back of my mind, was the thought that we had to get to know more people and here was a chance. I had reservations just the same. On this first day home with a new baby I felt weak and weepy. As with my other confinements, there was this dividing line of hospital and home, protection and you-are-on-your-own-now feeling, responsible for a new being. It wasn't until the births of my sixth and seventh babies that this problem was solved. They were born at home, in our own bedroom.

Afternoon tea in the Jacobs' prairie house with the rural ladies of Sandyhills and district, was very like afternoon tea with the rural ladies of the W.R.I. back home. Women the world over will always have things in common to talk about. My new baby and I brought a brightness to the occasion – something new to talk about, give advice on (they were all experts), tell their husbands about when they got back home in the evening. I didn't say a great deal. I listened and learned. They asked me what I thought of Sandyhills and the new hospital and how I liked the almost-new supermarket on the outskirts of town. However, like Betty Jacobs and other Canadians we had met, they seemed curiously uninterested in anything of my life that had gone before – weren't interested as to where I had come from or why. I suppose, to many, Scotland was just an uninteresting dot on the map. As far as they were concerned, here and now, was all there was or ever would be.

That evening I was very tired and burst into tears for no reason. Ronald was accustomed to this new-baby-syndrome by now and knew what to do. He put the boys to bed and saw that I went also.

In the summer days that followed Mahri-Louise spent a lot of the daylight hours outside. She lay in the shade of the cottonwood trees with a net over her pram to keep off the flies.

I also spent as much time as I could outside. Each morning I took my washing out, in the galvanised tub, to wash on the wooden platform at the door, with squirrels at my feet, birds at my head. There were, of course, also the unwelcome visitors – the flies, mosquitoes, wasps. The latter were attracted to the water and sometimes I had to beat a hasty retreat into the cabin to escape their potential barbed attacks. The flies and mosquitoes, as far as I could gather, held no serious threat to health and were not quite so numerous as I had been led to expect they might be. I asked Betty Jacobs about this one day.

"They're sure bad out in 'the sticks' proper," she said, "but Tom puts insect-repellent bombs into all the sloughs (water-holes) around. This destroys their breeding grounds, I guess."

I also asked her the names of the graceful butterflies that fluttered around my wash tub. Mostly she wasn't sure but she did know the name of my most uncommon common visitor. This butterfly was unmistakable and easy to describe – a Parisienne lady arrayed elegantly in black – a contrast to the brilliance of the sun, the brightness of the air.

"Mourning Cloak," she told me. How appropriate.

The boys spent most of the day outside that summer, often coming in only for meals. Tom Jacobs had dumped a load of sand near to our house for their benefit. A lot of the day was spent there, building and knocking down again. Quickly their young limbs grew brown and their hair bleached in the sun. They were happy. They didn't talk much about the country they had left behind, although from time to time they blurted out things that had happened at home. It seemed as if they weren't aware of how far away their old home was. Of the three boys, Michael missed it most of all. He was a child of few words so one couldn't be exactly sure what he was thinking but there had been a close bond between him and his grandmother and I knew he was missing her. I told the boys from time to time that one day granny and grandad would come in an aeroplane to visit them. Once, while crossing the yard to hang washing on the line, passing the sandpile, I came upon Michael standing all by himself looking up into the sky. He was so totally absorbed that he hadn't noticed me approaching. The other two boys had beetled off on hearing that loneliest of all sounds, the whistle of a prairie train, to stand at the picket fence and watch its long snake body trundle by. Michael, his attention for once otherwise diverted, hadn't moved. He stood, barefooted in the sand. His blue eyes overhung by slightly drooping lids, looked naturally sad. He gazed straight upward into a vast dome where, unmistakably, a plane, like a small silver ball, flew over us. I heard words from the child that seemed to echo the haunting sound of the Prairie Schooner.

"Is that you up there, granny?" he said.

On one of these sunlit days, shortly after the birth of Mahri-Louise, I made a conscious decision to start writing poetry. This was something I had hardly thought about since my childhood days. At fifteen I'd given up the idea completely. Poetry didn't seem to belong to everyday practical life and anyway who was I to think I could be a poet? I can't remember exactly why, out in this Westland, the decision to start writing again was taken – to alleviate the loneliness caused by the lack of adult companionship; to prevent me from brooding on an unforseeable tomorrow.

But mostly, I think, it was a compulsion to capture in words this sunlit land, entirely new to me – its birds, its butterflies, its animals, its special aura – and also my thoughts and feelings on this re-birth into a different place.

Apart from the bible and the encyclopaedias I had no books to go by and I certainly couldn't afford to buy any even if Sandyhills had boasted a book shop. But I had the music of half-remembered poems in my head – of Byron and Wordsworth, Tennyson and Shelley. I struggled with metre and rhyme and words while washing or cooking or feeding the baby until I got what I sought in as orderly a fashion as I could. I kept this up for over a year until life took off again and was filled with the chatter of other adults once more.

Much later, on the day that my seventh child went to school, in order to alleviate the sadness of the absence of childish feet around the house after seventeen years of their ceaseless patter, I took to cleaning out some long ignored drawers. From one of them I pulled out an old exercise book. It was bright orange in colour and in large, bold, black letters, proclaimed 'HUGE', which it wasn't. Underneath, in smaller letters, it said 10c and below that, 'Scribbler'. I looked inside. There were my Prairie poems.

I was in two minds as to whether to run downstairs and thrust the jotter hastily into the kitchen fire without so much as a glance or whether to tentatively read one or two. I was sure they would make me cringe with embarrassment at my inept attempts at poetry. To my surprise this was not the chief reaction. It was like looking over long forgotten photographs except that they seemed more real and immediate. They brought back to me vividly the things I had seen and how I had felt at the time. In these early prairie days, the actual trigger that released the first poem came from the elder of the Jacobs' two daughters. One day she burst into the cabin and energetically handed me a bunch of flowers.

"They grow wild," she told me, "I picked them for you."

They were, by far, the most colourful flowers I had seen since coming to Canada. There weren't many flowers around, wild or otherwise.

"They're called Brown-Eyed-Susans," she continued. "Do you like them?" Like them! – after a winter without flowers I thought they were beautiful and aptly named, deep brown eyes looking at me from a colourful sun of petals. They brought grace and wildness into the house.

Gradually I took all these lovely new names and words – Saskatoon, Gopher, Garter Snake, Grackle, Chipmunk, Coyote, Oriole, Mourning Cloak. I tried to string them together coming up with rather extravagant and arcane verses, not all that good, but with the power to bring back memories that gave me the confidence to write at a later date.

> Oriole – Emperor on wing
> Oft from his leafy throne will sing
> I love each glorious golden note
> Emerging from his deep dark throat

I wrote mostly of the things I saw around me that were new and also of the children. One day I wrote a lullaby for Mahri-Louise who, even although lying in the shade of the trees most of the time, grew as brown as a beechnut. Cradled in my arms, at bath time or feeding time or when for some reason she was crying, I used to sing it to her –

> The birds and the grasses far from the city
> Sing her a ditty
> Isn't she pretty?
> The sigh of the trees
> Like the sough of the seas
> Sooth to sleep my Mahri-Louise.

At a much later date, when I took up the writing of poetry more seriously, I wrote another poem about our home at Sandyhills.

> Born again
> Into fresh experience.
> Time stops a moment
> Beside these wood-shingled walls
> Of this small shack
> In my new wilderness:

Lets me catch up.
From a brazen sky
A cut-out bluebird drops,
Flies overhead.
A stray thought pulses the mind –
Colour must deepen with proximity.
Straggling cottonwoods
With bark on spindle trunks
Smooth, silver-white
And ragged at the edges,
Give small pattern to this extensive plain:
The straight-snake train
Slides past the tall grain tower,
That apostrophies the vast near-empty page,
And blows the world's most hollow sound:
All else is silent – still
Except for pale gold coyote
That lopes along like large Alsatian dog
And turns with curiosity
To watch a stranger species
Lonely in *his* land.

Chapter 16

Twisters

Life did not go altogether smoothly in that first month after my return from hospital. What with looking after Ronald and the boys in these primitive conditions, and breast feeding the baby, it took all the energy I had. By night time I was often exhausted and to make matters worse my wretched tooth started aching again. At the first opportunity I made an appointment with the dentist, but as in Red Deer, I was told I would have some time to wait.

Ronald was very busy again. I only saw him to speak to when he came in for a hurried meal or at night when all he wanted to do was sleep. He mentioned from time to time a pain in his chest. He made light of it saying it had all to do with the long hours of work and living at what was for us a high altitude

"I'll be all right," he joked," when I get used to this high living!"

I was concerned just the same, but he wouldn't hear of going to the doctor. All I could do was to give him as little worry and work as possible when he did come home.

The huge yard in front of our house was a hive of activity these days. Now, with seeding over, the men were making silage for the winter. The silage pits were close to the feed lots at the opposite side of the yard. Tom Jacobs, as always, demanded fast work. Tractors and trailers raced in from the prairie loaded up with cut grass which was quickly deposited in the pits allowing the tractors to roar out again for more. The grass was sometimes so dry that a hose pipe had been erected to sprinkle it with water in order to make it ferment properly. From time to time when the grass became high and unstable over the edge of the pit, a tractor had to run on top of it to tread it down. Ronald usually got this job. It was a dicey occupation at the best of times but with the grass wet and slippery and Jacobs always demanding speed it was downright dangerous. One false move and the tractor could easily slip over the edge and turn turtle.

"Can't help thinking," said Ronald to me one evening, "Jacobs would just love to see me take a tumble on that pit one of these times. How he would laugh. He's an odd man."

Odd indeed to be so careless with the men's lives and so careful with the children's. They weren't allowed anywhere near the pits while the silage was being made. His orders were strict. The children listened. He was a man to be obeyed.

One day I saw little Mandy Jacobs running across the yard again. I had just finished feeding Mahri-Louise, had laid her down in the pram and was looking out the window to see where the boys had got to. They weren't with her. She was on her own and came running up the steps quite out of breath.

"What is it?" I said in alarm.

"Mum says could you come over to the house. Something has happened to Ron."

I momentarily froze with fear – the pain in his chest – tractors turning turtle! Asking Mandy to keep an eye on the baby I flew over to the farmhouse looking neither to right nor left. The Jacobs' big Pontiac was purring at the door. As I arrived the screen door of the farmhouse had just banged shut behind Betty Jacobs and she was walking towards the car. I saw Ronald slumped in the front seat. Running up to him I asked,

"What's wrong? – goodness me what's wrong?" Ronald looked at me out of eyes filled with pain.

"The water," was all he could say.

"He'll be all right," butted in Betty Jacobs trying to calm the fear in my eyes. "He's been drinking hose pipe water. That water's sure no good to anyone – too much alkali. I'm taking him into hospital. They'll give him an injection for the pain and probably keep him in overnight. I guess Ronald didn't know about the water."

I felt like saying, well for goodness sake could someone not have told him, but refrained. That was the problem. There were dangers but we didn't know what they were and no one thought to tell us.

118

I put my hand through the open window and took Ronald's hand in mine. It was tense and clammy. He could hardly speak the pain was so bad but characteristically told me not to worry, that he'd be all right. How I wished I'd had my Canadian licence and could get into our car with the kids and follow them into hospital. Betty again assured me he would be OK. She had seen this sort of thing before. Never in all my years of nursing had I seen eyes so full of pain as Ronald's were now.

"As soon as I come back I'll come and tell you how he is," she said.

It was quite some time before Betty Jacobs returned. To me it seemed a lifetime but the news was good.

"They gave him an injection as soon as he got there," she said. "He's feeling better already but they're keeping him overnight, as I thought they would. I'll go for him in the morning."

Greatly relieved I thanked her for her kindness. Just the same, I spent a sleepless night trying to keep at bay all the dire possibilities of Ronald's condition, although I had no cause to disbelieve what Betty had told me.

Next morning, true to her word, Ronald arrived back, pain quite gone but looking tired and shaken.

"He's to take two to three days off," Betty instructed.

When she left, Ronald said,

"I'll bet Jacobs is hopping mad at me being off work."

"Never mind about him," I said. "It's his fault. He should have warned you about the water."

"He's an odd fellow," Ronald continued. "I just don't understand him. He saw me drinking from the hose yesterday but never said anything. It was such a hot day and making silage is so thirsty a job that I drank quite a lot. I couldn't come over to the house and have a drink – that would be considered a waste of time. Perhaps he thought I would just get a sore stomach and that would be funny and yet I don't know. There was one time, in the spring, I didn't tell you about. He was in a blind rage about something. He very nearly killed me. Let a machine down when he knew I was underneath it. Just got out in the nick of time. Perhaps he thinks it funny making me jump but sometimes I get the feeling it's more sinister than that. Don't worry about it though

– I'm pretty careful these days. And it's strange – he harms himself also – here I am – off for a few days when he most needs me."

I had been secretly worrying about Jacobs' moods but at the moment saw no good in making a fuss about it.

"I know you'll be careful," was all that I said, "and in one way the bad water was a good thing. You need a rest. Jacobs does work you and Adrian far too hard."

One thing that Ronald did during this unexpected break was to write to my mother – something he had been meaning to do for some time. He never told me what he wrote in the letter. Many years were to pass before I came across it quite by chance. I wrote to my mother and father frequently in those early days in Canada. Finding my letters interesting, they kept them all in a shoebox which I discovered while clearing out their home when in Scotland. I looked through it and came upon the letter Ronald had sent so long before. I paused – should I read it? Curiosity got the better of me. To begin with I was interested to read of Ronald's reactions to these times, and then moved and touched at the comments on my younger self.

Dear Mother, it began.

> I am having a few days off owing to a gastric complaint which has been painful but not serious. This has given me a little time in which to write to you.
> It has been a long journey and is not over yet for we are far from satisfied in our present position. It has taken time to recover from the changes. We needed a space of comparative peace and quiet to carry us through some of the rougher patches and get the feel of things. It takes a wee while to become oriented into a new environment. To begin with even the smallest things are unnerving. For example, in stores, it is not always obvious whether you are supposed to help yourself or be served or where to pay for the goods. It's so very different from home. I find even these small things can shake my confidence and make me diffident. It has, of course, not been easy coming to Canada, but we have overcome much together. Being together is

what makes it possible and helps to keep up our morale
– that is most important. Your letters have been a great
help in this respect.

Though the work is hard there are many compens-
ations – such as sunshine. Having a car also makes a big
difference to our lives. We were practically prisoners
without one.

We get the full local rate of pay which is not bad for
newcomers although farm work is very poorly paid.
However I have great hopes for the future although not
perhaps in farming. I do not know if we will ever make a
fortune but the chances are here and I mean to try.
That is the great thing – in Canada it is up to yourself.
So far, I have not regretted coming here and I don't
think I ever will. A period of waiting, doing at least one
season on a farm, is what is needed. Though we have
lived a fairly quiet life so far, as we get stronger we
mean to visit the few friends we have and make as many
new contacts as we can. There are great opportunities
here and so much to see. Why didn't we come before?
It is not the journey that is difficult, but overcoming the
inertia of a safe rut. This is easier to do when you are
younger. How much better would I have been to come
five or ten years ago.? At thirty four I am already too
old for some jobs. This is a young man's country.

The boys are fine and healthy – have enormous fun
running about the yard (no mud, stones or hills). The
Princess is in 'roaring' health and growing fast. I wish
you could see her.

I know you would love her.

I have not attempted to tell you all that is going on,
rather the thoughts in my head. Margaret gives you all
the news very adequately. She has been marvellous, as
it is not easy for her.

If anything, she has had the heavy end of the stick.
In moments of weakness, as now, with this gastric
trouble, due to drinking bad water, it is more difficult to
see what we are striving for. Then I look around me

and see my children delighting in new surroundings –
new games. What an adventure it is for them. I look
over at my beloved Margaret, her dark hair pulled back
from her pretty Scottish face. She is nursing our
Princess Mahri-Louise, her eyes filled with maternal
love and pride. What strength she has bringing our
newborn into a new and difficult land – giving her life to
be a mother and a wife. Never complaining about our
hardships, instead showing great spirit and resilience
and most of all hope. Suddenly it becomes clear that
everything that is dear to me is in this cabin and if we
have managed this far things can only get better which
gives me an immense feeling of well-being and
satisfaction. How lucky I am.
Many thanks for all the interest you both have taken in
our activities. This spurs us on to fresh efforts.
Love, Ronald

Not long after Ronald had gone back to work another unexpected
event occurred which, in retrospect, turned out to be more
amusing than serious. On afternoons when I was feeling
especially tired, I tried to have a snooze for half an hour after
feeding Mahri-Louise. Usually wee Ronnie had a nap in the
afternoons around this time also but the other two refused. They
were big boys now they told me. However Richard became my
ally and promised to keep an eye on the mischievous Michael.
He would come and tell me if he was doing anything bad, he
said. I found him most reliable. After half an hour my watchdog
would creep quietly into my bedroom being careful not to waken
the baby. He would then pat me gently on the shoulder and
whisper,

"Does the clock say it's time to get up yet, Mummy?"

One afternoon I left Richard and Michael playing happily with
the girls and was just dropping off to sleep when I became aware
of Richard in the room.

"Mummy, Mummy!" he was blurting out through his tears,
"prickle beasties, prickle beasties!"

I shot out of bed to discover Richard covered from head to

foot in small ants. They had been out playing in the wood beside the house and he had inadvertently walked over an ant hill in the cloth slippers that the boys wore. How he had got so many on him, I shall never know. There were hundreds of them, crawling on his face, arms, legs, everywhere. It took quite some time to brush them all off. Meanwhile the girls came in with Michael who stood watching me with a fascinated horror in his eyes. He came closer and closer as I brushed the ants off Richard almost as though drawn by what he most feared.

"Keep away!" I warned him, "or you'll get them on you as well."

Too late! One solitary ant landed on Michael and began to crawl slowly up his leg. The screams that came from the ant's new host could have been heard far across the prairie.

Richard seemed none the worse of his infestation and he and Michael were soon all smiles again. I gave them a picnic along with the girls, out on the sunny deck, of chocolate milk and biscuits from the cookie jar. Mandy told me these ants were not dangerous. She had had them on her on occasions.

"It's probably the cloth slippers that attracted them," she said.

As far as I could find out there wasn't much that was dangerous in these parts, but I couldn't be sure. I had been warned about poison ivy in Canada but Betty Jacobs said there was none around that she knew about. In fact, she didn't think there was any in Alberta.

However there was one thing that she hadn't warned me about and it happened one day when she and the girls were away shopping in Sandyhills and the men were all back out on the prairie attending to the wheat crop which was throwing a greenness over the land. This time I really did get a fright.

As usual it was a lovely sunbright morning. I was out on the wooden deck washing clothes. There wasn't a cloud in the sky and if there was disturbance in the air, I certainly didn't notice it. The boys were down on the other side of the yard engrossed in some game or other. Suddenly I heard a tremendous noise resembling a fleet of heavy bombers approaching. This was surprising as we saw very few planes. Suddenly the huge noise seemed to be passing me by but at a distance. Where I stood nothing was happening at all. The sun was shining, everything was still. I looked towards the boys on the other side of the yard. There I saw total confusion. A wall of swirling dust had arisen and within its frightening clutches the boys, like so much jetsam caught in a whirlpool, were turning and falling screaming and crying, a massive wind lifting them off their feet. Black terror enveloped me as I involuntarily sprinted over the yard, got hold of the boy's hands and pulled them out of the narrow fierce path of the wind. I was trembling from head to foot. The boys were thickly covered in dust. They were badly frightened but, apart from a few bruises, unhurt. As suddenly as it came the wind went, pursuing its furious way across the prairie towards the Rocky Mountains.

"A 'twister', a 'dust devil'," Betty Jacobs called it later when listening with sympathy to my tale. "I guess we get them from time to time. They sure are nasty if you happen to be in their path."

The boys didn't take long to get over their fright. I bathed them and again out came the cookie jar and the chocolate milk. Soon they were laughing and waiting with impatience for Dad to come in for lunch so that they could tell him about 'the big wind'!

Chapter 17

Homesteaders' Parade

"Breakfast in the streets of Sandyhills," Mandy told me.

"Bacon and pancakes cooked on barbecues set up on sidewalks," Susan enlarged on the event.

"Afterwards a long parade through the town with everyone dressed up, decorated trucks, horses – lots of horses, music and, and . . ." Mandy hurried on before her sister was able to get a word in, "and then the wildest stampede in all Alberta."

Mandy was a loyalist when it came to anything that happened around and about Sandyhills. She was also an enthusiast, one who made everything sound so good that it bred heightened anticipation in others. As far as she was concerned Sandyhills was the best place on earth.

"It sure is top town around these parts," she told me with pride one day. "It has paved streets and traffic lights and no other town has that all the way to Edmonton. "Also," she continued, "it's real, real old – all of fifty years. That's why the stampede is to be extra special this year, the town is celebrating its fiftieth anniversary."

The morning dawned clear and bright as it usually does in Alberta. In this respect how different from home. Here families could really plan an outdoor event and be pretty certain the weather would stay fair. For all of us at Jacobs' place, the atmosphere was charged with excitement. The boys were up early. We intended going into Sandyhills as soon as possible. I thought breakfast in the streets was a lovely idea. I could smell the bacon sizzling on the barbecues, see the foamy yellow pancakes running with maple syrup. However an unplanned change of events kept us from this ritual.

Principally it was Adrian who was responsible for the change in plans. Back home in Somerset he had taken part in amateur dramatics. In a good-humoured way he was a bit of a show off and a clown and this hobby suited his extrovert nature. His aptitude for public entertaining had been somewhat thwarted since coming to Canada and he was determined to make use of every opportunity to redress the balance. He wanted to take part in the parade but he needed a partner. He had thought it all out. Being round-faced, over six feet and broad with it, he thought he would make an excellent oversized 'baby'. All he needed was a slightly smaller 'mother'. At the last moment his more sober friend Phil on the neighbouring farm, who had never been too happy with the idea, refused to do it. In desperation on the morning of the parade, Adrian came over to our cabin to ask Ronald if he would oblige. Rather to Adrian's surprise, in spite of faith in his own persuasive powers, Ronald agreed. I was surprised also but didn't try to stop him. I was only too happy to see a little of the old humorous Ronald I knew return. He was a born comedian with a natural power to make people laugh. Adrian sensed a kindred spirit.

The Jacobs were all for Adrian's plan. They liked the thought of people from Jacobs' place taking part in the event. It would no doubt give them a certain prestige in the community. In fact, I suspected it might have been at Betty Jacobs' instigation that Adrian came round to ask Ronald. Perhaps, with her own quiet sense of humour plus a certain woman's intuition, she sensed the rightness of it. At all events she had everything prepared for the 'dressing up' over in her house.

Ronald and Adrian disappeared while I gave the boys breakfast and fed Mahri-Louise. Half an hour later they re-appeared in unrecognisable form. I didn't know them and neither did the boys. All of the big hulk of Adrian was cocooned in a muslin dress, all sprigs and little flowers. He had a bonnet to match which had a frilly edge and was tied round his blue-shadowed chin with a pink ribbon. Betty Jacobs must have made the complete ensemble especially for the occasion. Ronald wore a knee-length dress (presumably belonging to Betty) with a three-cornered piece of material tied at the nape of the neck and slung where his bosom should have been, to make up for any deficiency in shape. On his head, at a perky angle, sat one of Betty's hats, festooned with feathers. However, Ronald had refused to take off his trousers and boots, partly because he didn't want to and partly because he knew that with them on it made the image even funnier. Both of them had clown faces made up by Adrian who had had considerable practice in the art. 'Mother' had thick lips with a distinct downward swing while 'baby's' were thick also with a definite upward swing, almost touching round feverish spots, high on the cheek bones denoting the unmistakable sign of teething. 'Mother' was armed with nappy pins, nappies, rattles, bottles of milk and juice – all things necessary for a day at the stampede with baby. Phil, although refusing to be mother, had deigned to be 'father' – but straight – no funny stuff. He was dressed in blue jeans, fringed western shirt, lariat tie and ten gallon-hat.

"That's Adrian, your Dad and Phil," I said to the boys as the three came over the yard towards us. (You could have fooled me but I knew it must be them.)

"Aren't they funny?" I said, thinking that the boys would enjoy the joke as much as I did.

To my astonishment their reaction was quite different. Michael burst out crying and tears ran down Richard's cheeks in sympathy. Ronnie had a sober expression on his round chubby face. I crouched down to their level.

"You recognise Phil," I said, "and the other two are Adrian and your Dad dressed up as clowns – funny men!"

They stopped crying but I could see by their solemn faces that they weren't going to be so easily appeased. They didn't like to see their Dad playing the fool dressed up as a woman. This change had upset their secure world. Ronald, Adrian, Phil and I all tried to get them to laugh but we didn't make much headway and time was short.

"We'll go on ahead in Adrian's car. The parade starts at eleven," Ronald said, looking at his watch, "and it's ten thirty now. We'll need to hurry."

In the meantime the Jacobs had been trying to fit an old pram, once presumably used to wheel Mandy and Susan about the yard, into the back of Adrian's car. They were having a struggle but after removing the wheels and the handle, managed to do it. When the three men and the pram were safely aboard, the car took off with a screech of brakes and a souped up roar from the exhaust, flinging out a thick screen of dust and a grapeshot of stones as they went. I had just got my Canadian driving licence and followed more soberly at a safe distance. The boys in the back seat were still somewhat subdued but brightened up when we arrived at Sandyhills. No one could mistake the feeling in the air that this was indeed a special day.

I parked the car as near to the centre of town as I could and the boys helped me out with Mahri-Louise's fold-down pram. Soon we found a suitable bit of sidewalk among the waiting people from which to watch the parade. It had started, we were informed, but it would be some time before it reached us. You could feel the excitement in the crowd. There were dogs barking, babies crying, children jumping up and down with the sheer joy of living.

We heard the procession long before we could see it, and then it was upon us. Before our eyes passed every conceivable type of decorated truck plus hill-billy bands strumming out western music, lines of marching girls in short frilly skirts led by proud and prancing majorettes skilfully twirling batons. There were also battalions of cowboys and girls in western rig, riding on horseback and then came a long section of the parade given to scenes from the homesteaders on trek from a not-so-distant past. The wooden carts, drawn by two oxen, were the real thing. In front of each hung a large cowbell, a musical accompaniment belonging to a different era. I was standing out of time watching a scene from yesterday passing in front of me.

The men, women and children taking part in this tableau were so natural that for a long time afterwards I wondered if they really were made-up or did some sections of the community still dress like this? The women wore simple dresses reaching down to their ankles. Since coming to Canada I hadn't seen women thus dressed but had heard rumours of communities of folk living in the old way with names I hadn't heard back home – Mennonites, Huttenites, Dukhobors, religious groups who lived away from other people in communities of their own. They lived more or less by their own laws and customs and because they practiced communal living, helping each other and being thrifty, were amassing land. Their communities were becoming larger and larger to the point where the Canadian government was getting worried about their potential strength.

On the crowded sidewalks today, however, most men and women of all ages and sizes wore tight fitting jeans, tartan shirts and stetsons. Some figures were just not suitable for tight-fitting jeans, especially among the woman. It did not seem to matter how fat the lady might be, she looked quite unselfconscious dressed like this. It was the correct costume for the day. I began to feel out of place in my cool blue and white summer dress.

Shortly after the homesteaders had passed I heard faint echoes of a different sound. It came closer and closer till I recognised it as laughter. It came sweeping up the street, of this dusty western town in swirls and dancing gusts in much the same erratic way as the wind whirled through the barley back home. The boys heard it.

"Why are the people laughing?" Richard said, craning his neck through the crowd in an attempt to see further up the street.

"Perhaps it is because your Dad and Adrian are coming." I replied. "Now remember to clap."

In the general excitement the boys seemed to have got over their adverse feelings about Daddy being a clown and waited eagerly for something they knew about and in a way was theirs. The sound of laughter increased until suddenly it was amongst us, lifting and roaring, jumping from one to the other. Infectious laughter that promoted more laughter.

The clowns were funny, there was no doubt about that. They didn't just march in the procession as so many other participants had done, they fooled and clowned all the way. An inept and idiosyncratic 'mother' and a difficult and mischievous 'baby', the spontaneous work of two born artistes who knew naturally and exactly what to do to make people laugh. Phil had dropped into the role of fall guy which suited his lesser but necessary talents.

The little prairie town rocked with laughter. The boys now were laughing also. People had handkerchiefs out and were drying their eyes long after the clowns had passed and the laughter trailed off into the prairie. I listened to the comments and questions around me – "Never seen anything so funny!" – "Who are those guys?" – "How come we've not heard of them before?" They were the unknown quantity – the complete surprise in a land that, as far as I could see, was a little lacking in fun and humour. Perhaps living in this land was too serious an occupation for jokes.

Later we learned from Adrian that the Jacobs had been delighted with the act and the response to it. They were pleased to have had a secret hand in it all and to be the only ones with the answer to the question – "Who are the clowns?"

The crowd was gathering all the time in this piece of prairie cordoned off for the event. It was a true family day out. There were children everywhere. Some parents had brought their families of ten or twelve kids and granny as well. The latter also was dressed, more often than not, in a stetson and jeans, an astonishing sight to someone from Scotland in the fifties. Now that it was past midday it had become really hot and tartan shirts and fringed jackets were peeled of to reveal t-shirts with all sorts of western motifs on them. This was the garb of the women as well as the men. Some of the ladies had shorts on. They had had them on under their jeans. They had come prepared for the heat. Again it seemed of no consequence the size of the lady, summer had come and after nine months of winter she was going to make the most of it.

The arena where the events were to be held had a high fence round it. There was another fence at some distance from the arena that surrounded all of us spectators. High also, but not so high that we could not see what lay beyond. At one end lay the large grid of inconsequential shops and houses that was Sandyhills, and at the other the wide open prairie. A light wind was blowing making the bright sunlit air ever so slightly dusty and sending large light balls of tumbleweed scuttling across the prairie to be caught against the fence. Every now and then a bluebird would come soaring in towards us from the sky. It was all very new to Ronald and me and all very exciting. The events of the afternoon were about to begin. We moved closer into the ringside, pram and all. The boys got right up to the fence. Canadians were kind to children and saw that they got a good viewing point. The boys' eyes became glued to what was happening in the ring.

The wild horse-riding event began the proceedings. Many of the horses taking part had been especially bred and trained in the Rocky Mountains to buck from the moment they were born. It was pure lottery which horse the competitor got. He pulled a ticket with a number that told him which one he was allocated. There was one horse in Alberta at that time, called Blue Mountain – the roughest toughest one of all. Every cowboy feared getting it. The goal of the competition was for the cowboy to stay on the back of his bucking bronco as long as possible and for at least eight seconds.

"The longest eight seconds in the world" one cowboy told me. "Once I pulled Blue Mountain – the meanest horse in all Canada. Just my luck. All I remember was catapulting out of the chute and then clutching a fistful of dust."

We watched them as they were let into the ring, the horses heads down, heels up in the sky. They knew every trick in the book for unseating riders and didn't hesitate to use them. The cowboys knew all the moves also and were expert in moving into what they anticipated the horse would try next but I wondered how they could stay on any of the horses for one second let alone eight.

The roping of calves was the next event. The calves had been herded straight from the open range and had hardly, if ever, seen man or horse before. They were wild, nervous and fleet of foot. The aim of the cowboy was to lasso one with his lariat while galloping through the ring, then jump off his horse and tightly bind his captive all in the fastest time possible.

"Six seconds – that's what they have to beat to make a new record," I overheard some one say in the crowd. "But I sure don't think they'll do it today."

We watched them let loose the calves into the ring and then in came the cowboys – man and horse moulded together. The art of swinging a lariat (it was never called a lasso in Alberta) looked simplicity itself but I knew what endless practice and

131

usage it must take to be able to catch, with such fine judgement and accuracy, these madly running calves. It was a spectacular sight to watch them catch the calf, jump from the horse with the speed of light and truss up the four feet of the struggling beast. No one did it in six seconds that day but one or two were not far off it.

Other events were equally as breathtaking. Texan bulls were let into the ring. They were all lean and rangy. Some so thin that you could count every rib in their sinuous bodies. They had long mean pointed horns. They were allowed to run round the ring for a while and then in came the mounted cowboys. Their task was to get as close to one of these beasts as possible, get hold of a horn, jump onto its neck and by a clever manoeuvre tip the beast over with four feet off the ground. I was glad that this task was accomplished fairly early on. The first to do so was the winner – the contest was over. I was relieved, I could see it was a dangerous occupation.

"Dangerous," said a cowboy. "What you'll do when you're young! I've sure left some flesh on different stamping grounds but there is one thing that no one could ever persuade me to try and that is to ride a Brahmin bull. For me, certain death. They'd kill you in a minute."

That was the next event – Brahmin bull baiting. I shut my eyes at this one. I'd had enough and Mandy had told me this was the most dangerous event of all. Sometimes a cowboy was killed. I heard the ohs and ahs of the crowd, felt the mounting tension around me and then at last the cheering.

"You can open your eyes now, Mummy. It's over and there's nobody deaded," said Richard.

A later event was a little less dangerous, perhaps, and certainly amusing. That was the wild cow milking. The cows were let into the ring, the mounted cowboys cantering after them in pairs. One cowboy concentrated on throwing his lariat round a cow's neck and restraining it as best he could while his partner jumped of his horse holding a bottle and procured spurts of milk into his bottle from a madly thrashing cow. Not easy! Quite a bit of clowning went on, some cowboys getting more spurts of milk over their faces than into the bottle. There was loud cheering as one after the other cowboy rushed to the winning post to get their few spurts of milk accurately measured. The winners were the team who had the most milk in their bottle in the fastest time.

I actually got the biggest fright just towards the end of this competition. Suddenly one of the cows was rushing towards us from inside the ring. I could see what it was meaning to do.

"Watch out!" Ronald and I yelled simultaneously to the boys. It took a flying leap and cleared the fence just missing us and others beside us. On it barged and taking another flying leap cleared the second barrier also. My heart was still thumping madly when I heard a calm voice drawling from the loud speaker in the ring

"That one's sure in a hurry. I guess it just can't wait to get back to the open range."

In the evening the big event was chuckwagon racing. Chuckwagons were covered carts, replicas of those used long ago for carrying food across the prairies by homesteaders on trek. It was exciting to watch. Each team was all out to win. There were quite a few collisions although no major damage ensued. In the middle of it all, a chill wind blew in from the Arctic reminding us that it might be high summer in Alberta, but that there was little to stop a wind coming straight from the North Pole. The boys were getting tired and irritable and Mahri-Louise hungry. We made for the car. While I was feeding Mahri-Louise, Ronald and I talked over the day's events.

"What now?" I asked, "head for the open prairie?"

Instinctively I knew Ronald didn't feel like going home just yet.

"What's in your mind?" I queried,

"There's a party planned after dark in the supermarket. We are invited and the kids too, of course."

Darkness fell sooner and more quickly than it would have on a Scottish summer evening. In the back of the car Ronnie and Michael had fallen asleep. Richard was, as usual, as wide awake as an owl. Mahri-Louise nodded off as I cradled her in my arms. I placed her gently in the pram that now, without its wheels, served as a carrycot. It fitted nicely over the front seat.

Ronald drove close to the door of the supermarket and he took Richard with him. I waited behind for a while to make sure the others were sound asleep. Bob, the manager of the supermarket, who was giving the party, had been very good to us ever since we first arrived in Sandyhills. He was a comparative newcomer himself. Ronald and he had taken an instant liking to each other. Bob was a pleasant man with a good sense of humour. The day we arrived in Sandyhills it was early closing day and all the stores were shut but he had opened up the supermarket especially for us. Since then, each Saturday the supermarket was kept open longer than usual.

"Only for you folks," he would tell us every Saturday after our shopping was done, when along with one or two others of the store's employees, we had a little party – a dram for the menfolk, cake and popcorn for me and the children. Also Bob never let us leave the store without some candy for the kids and food that would soon be beyond its sell-by date. Only the previous Saturday, he had given us several bunches of celery, three or four pounds of apples, four cauliflowers, a bunch of bananas, a melon and potatoes. He had a compassionate heart. We never put on a poor face but reading between the lines, he knew it was not easy for us to manage on the wages we got.

On that evening after the stampede I joined the party for a short time. To the melodic strains of a guitar plucking out western tunes, we danced up and down the aisles – past cans of peas, carrots, sweetcorn, past watermelons, onions, cabbages, past huge boxes of detergent, high towers of toilet paper. Miraculously, while we were there, no great pyramids came tumbling down on top of us.

Soon we left the throng of cheerful dancing people and the music of guitar and mouth organ. I had always liked Western music but tonight I was completely captivated. As we drove home under a sky thick with stars, I started to sing.

> Give me land, lots of land
> In the prairies that I love,
> Don't fence me in:
> Give me land, lots of land

Neath the starry skies above,
Don't fence me in . . .

I sang until I ran out of words. From nowhere, it seemed, a stray
thought came into my head saying . . .

"This is all very well, this seduction by the new, but you
mustn't forget the old – your heritage, the land of your birth and
all that you are. You must try to give the children something of
that."

Ronald, who had been singing along with me, was silent now
also, concentrating on driving along the rutty tracks. Mahri-Louise
lay in my arms, half awake, half asleep. As we drove closer to
our clapboard shack the night became punctuated with the howl
of the coyotes and I found myself crooning to my youngest child,
Canadian by birth, a song completely alien to this strange land.

Oh Rowan Tree, oh Rowan Tree
Thou'lt aye be dear tae me
Entwined thou art
Wi' mony ties
o' hame and infancy. . .

135

Chapter 18

Romance in the Air

One day not long after the stampede, I was sitting in the living room comfortably curled up on the window seat. Ronald had made it for me with bits of wood he had found. I had padded it out with some unwanted material given to me by Betty Jacobs and covered it with curtain material brought from home. The rays from an afternoon sun streamed through the thin glass that kept the black flies from entering the house. Mahri-Louise was asleep in her pram. The boys were outside playing with Mandy and Susan. I had seized the opportunity, while it was quiet, to write a long letter to my mother. Eventually I laid down my pen and looked out of the window.

Perhaps I had become distracted by an unexpected sound – galloping hooves pounding on gravel. Curious, I craned my neck to see further down the road. A cloud of dust was approaching. Suddenly it was right outside my window. The dust settled to reveal a girl on a horse. I was hardly prepared for this apparition. The girl's long tawny hair settled round her shoulders as she patted the sweating neck of the horse, then she jumped from its back, tied it to the picket and with one hand on the end post jumped over the fence clearing it easily. Between the teeth of this lithe and handsome girl I noticed what looked like a letter. She made her way round the side of our cabin to its only door which faced on to the yard. I went to meet her and ask her in. Her dark eyes had the soft glow of someone in love. I was struck by her stance and colouring. She told me her name was Gloria which seemed to fit her perfectly. She handed me the letter.

"I'd sure be glad if you could give this to Adrian."

"Certainly," I said, too taken by surprise to say much more. Not that she gave me time. Before I could find words she had

136

leapt over the fence again and was on her horse. Down the trail they galloped leaving only dust and a memory.

By the time Ronald returned for tea I had a lovely romance going, everything cut and dried. When Adrian came over later we teased him.

"You've been quick off your mark, you're a quiet one," I said as I handed him the letter.

He took it all in his good humoured stride and seemed pleased. Later he told us about Gloria.

"Her parents have a quarter section not far from here," he said. "She is one of a big family. I couldn't say exactly how many. Everytime I go there seems to be one I haven't seen before!" A distressed look came into Adrian's usually cheerful countenance.

"I wouldn't have believed people could be so poor. They've nothing to show for all their years of hard work. They've very little furniture and their curtains on windows and doors are pieces of sacking sewn together. Last weekend two of her kid brothers came with us in the car to Sandyhills. I had some cakes that had been in the back window for weeks. They were hard, dusty and stale. I'd forgotten all about them. The boys wolfed them down as though they were fresh from the oven. Gloria is the eldest of the kids. She works hard in the house and the fields – never complains!"

After that first quick visit we saw a lot of Gloria. Quite often of a summer evening she would ride over to Jacobs' place to be with Adrian. Sometimes she gave him lessons in horse riding. These were hilarious. Everyone went into the yard to watch. Gloria had ridden from as far back as she could remember. Adrian had never ridden at all except perhaps a donkey on the beach. He was not the bravest of mortals, nor the most apt pupil, but he never shirked the challenge of trying something new.

Gloria's horse was, to say the least of it, spirited. First time round Adrian mounted with a certain trepidation which the horse felt right away and took off with a suddenness that had Adrian thrown on the ground in seconds. However Adrian's good-natured bravado, rather than his love of horses, made him try again and again until gradually the horse learned to accept this raw recruit and Adrian learned to ride cowboy style. Jacobs, perhaps more than any of us, enjoyed watching these riding sessions. A young strong Englishman being thrown off a horse made him roar with laughter.

There was one big difference between Jacobs and Adrian. Adrian didn't mind being laughed at. Being a born showman he probably wasn't so inept as he made out and played it up a bit to the point of risking getting hurt. Jacobs couldn't bear being laughed or criticised in any way. Jacobs also had a horse – a beautiful mare, the colour of summer clouds, called Lady. She lived in the paddock beyond the poplars.

Gloria loved horses and when she was at Jacobs' place would wander over to the paddock and attract Lady to the fence side. She always had some tit-bit for her in her pocket. Lady wouldn't come to everyone. Being ridden seldom she had grown wild and flighty. We had heard that she was used only once or twice a year to ride the range – a sort of common grazing stretching for miles that Jacobs and Cameron, his neighbour, owned between them.

Secretly both Ronald, who didn't like horses, and Adrian who feared them, were worried in case they would get the job. As it turned out Jacobs went himself to muster cattle taking with him Elmer, a cowboy who had come down from the north with his horse for summer work. They went off very early one morning, along with their neighbour and his cowboy, prepared for a day on the range. About midday Jacobs arrived back all by himself and limping badly. There was no sign of Lady although next morning she was back in her paddock as usual.

We never did hear what happened that day. The only hint we ever got that all had not gone according to plan, was from Mandy who told us next time we saw her that "Dad says Lady sure doesn't like her tummy tickled by willows."

Gloria told us more about Jacobs. How no one in the district would work for him because of his tantrums and that he loved his horse so much that he would let no one else ride her. She was indeed a beautiful animal with an intelligent eye and a graceful arching neck. I am sure, also, she had a sense of humour.

One evening Gloria told us an amusing incident concerning

Lady and her master. At Halloween the young folk in Alberta went in for a night of high spirited mischief. This was a recognised custom in the Province, a time when, to a certain extent, youth was allowed its head. Sometimes however, things could get out of control. Jacobs, not top of the popularity poll among the young men, had had trouble in the past and took every possible precaution to protect his property. The previous halloween, Gloria told us (and she had inside information as two of her brothers were mixed up in the mischief), Jacobs had gathered all his implements and tractors together in the yard. Whereupon he switched on all his powerful outside lights (fixed up especially for Halloween) and had sat up all night, watching from his bedroom window to see that nothing went amiss. However he had forgotten about Lady. The paddock where she lived was beyond the bright circle of light. In the morning, much to Jacobs' fury, he found her painted pink.

There were one or two evenings when Gloria arrived and the men had barely the energy to say 'hi' to her. On these days they had been engaged in the onerous task of shifting grain. When we were at Jacobs place there was a surplus of grain being grown in the prairies. Farmers had real trouble in selling it. The government, in order to bring some fairness into the situation, worked out a scheme whereby each farmer, according to his acreage, was allocated a day now and again when he could shift as much grain as he could possibly manage to the huge railway silo for shipment to the outer world. On that important day the men were out at the crack of dawn shovelling grain to the augers. These were long hollow tubes with moving spirals inside that levered the grain up into waiting trucks. On that day they got minimum time off for meals working until dusk when the silo closed down. It was a hard job shovelling to the augers for a short time. For a whole day with barely a break it was back-breaking. By the finish the men were exhausted. Never the most robust of men, I marvelled at Ronald's stamina. Oddly enough, although complaining of heightened pain in his chest, he seemed to stand the strain better than the younger and more stoutly built Adrian. After these sessions Adrian's whole body shook from head to foot.

Chapter 19

Visits to Sandyhills

Every Saturday evening without fail we went shopping, baby and all. Sandyhills was the metropolis upon which we all descended. Jacobs let Ronald off work at 4pm and after he had eaten, washed and changed, we all bundled into the car.

The boys were always excited about these evening excursions. The stores remained open longer than on weekdays and everyone for miles around came to town – farmers and hired hands alike. Everyone mixed with everyone else, the rich and the struggling. People treated each other as equals much more so than in rural towns back home in the fifties. I revelled in the atmosphere.

Saturday was definitely the family night out. Canada, in her attempt to fill up the wide open spaces, encouraged the bearing of children. Consequently there were some large families about. On Saturday evenings the streets were always busy. Quite the opposite from what it had been like on the afternoon I went into hospital to have Mahri-Louise. On Saturdays there was always an air of festivity, which increased as the days grew warmer. Parties in the supermarket ceased. The evenings were so pleasant that most people wanted to be outside parading up and down the sidewalks – seeing and being seen by others. Mostly everyone knew everyone else and we were getting to know a few people.

Our shopping completed we would sit up on high stools at the bar of an ice cream parlour and order ice cream floats. Then we would drift outside again into the warm air.

It was noisy outside with the chatter of people and the sound of traffic. Many of the cars on the road were old bangers owned by young men, their windscreens pitted, their silencers removed to make them roar more loudly. Sometimes a young girl was driving. I remember one occasion particularly well. I heard behind me the screech of sudden breaking and a strident female voice shouting,

"Take your God-damn beer and git out!"

Whereupon the car door flew open and a cowboy rolled at my feet. Several cans of beer came flying after him. One almost hit me. The cowboy got up, dusted himself down, and with a string of oaths picked up the cans of beer that had rolled into the gutter. Apart from us, no one seemed to take much notice so we assumed it was a usual occurrence.

Sometimes after the stores closed and darkness began to thicken, along with other families we made for the outdoor cinema. When first confronted with a huge silver screen stuck in the middle of nowhere I wondered what possible use it could have. Loosely fenced in from the prairie, it stood facing orderly rows of car-high posts. Because it stood in an otherwise featureless plain, it looked tall and impressive and could be seen for miles. The procedure, after entering the field, was to drive up to a vacant post, drop the appropriate coins into a slot provided, unhook a microphone and take it into the car through the window.

Michael and Ronnie were excited by the moving pictures on the screen but very quickly fell asleep. Richard, on the other hand, never got sleepy. He watched the screen assiduously and refused to consider leaving as long as there was a flicker on it.

I remember, one night, longing for *Sinbad the Sailor* to end. I was tired and didn't care for this kind of picture at the best of times but these grotesque creations of the imagination, prancing on the screen and intruding into the car, had a way of demanding attention. I would much rather have watched the stars in the night sky.

Sometimes after these Saturday excursions I drove home. Ronald wanted me to get used to driving on gravel roads and on, what was for us the wrong side of the road. Having a licence to drive enabled me to go to the dentist under my own steam. The day for the appointment eventually arrived. From day one of our arrival in Canada, the removal of this troublesome tooth had been one of my main desires. I made it a policy not to ask Mrs Jacobs for help if I could possibly avoid it. However the day previous to my appointment she made a hurried visit to the cabin with a bundle of rhubarb, beet tops, and swisschard from her garden and I mentioned it.

"I'll look after Mahri-Louise for you if you like," she said. I accepted her offer gladly. "Sandyhills is sure lucky to have a good dentist," she added. "He's a pleasant, able man. He sure won't take long to pull your tooth."

Mrs Jacobs was rather like Mandy in that everyone and everything was good in Sandyhills. I reserved my judgement.

On the day of the appointment I wasn't feeling well. I had become used to the constant ache of the errant tooth but on top of that I had caught a feverish cold from Ronald. He had been off for a couple of days in bed with a high temperature. Jacobs had been driving Adrian and Ronald hard again, re-seeding a quarter section of land. They were working night and day in temperatures that varied from tropical heat under a noonday sun to the Arctic coldness of midnight. I was feeling decidedly groggy on the day of the appointment. But, short of pneumonia, nothing would have stopped me from keeping it.

The boys came with me. I parked outside the surgery door and left them in the car with toys and books to look at and with strict instructions to Richard to look after his wee brothers.

"I won't be long," I assured them," and if you're all good, I'll buy you sweets when I come out."

Fortunately the dentist took me right away and I was soon in the chair. He examined the tooth touching it with a fine probe. The tooth screamed. He gave me an injection into the gum and left it for a while. When he came to touch it again the reaction was no better. Once more he gave me an injection and waited – no better!

"Uh huh!" he said after the failure of the third attempt. "Well, I'll give you the alternatives: – One, I put you on a course of penicillin to clear up the infection that is keeping the tooth from freezing. You can come back in a week and have it out; – Two, I'll yank it out now! The pain will be intense for a moment or two but that will be all the time it takes."

"I'll have it out now," I said after a short hesitation. I had my doubts about it coming out as easily as all that. I was a coward at the dentist but when would I get back?

"Ready?" he asked, sounding confident.

I nodded assent but my inner voice hadn't been wrong. The tooth wouldn't budge – no way! Then it began to break off in bits. I could hear it cracking.

"This is the toughest tooth I ever came across," the dentist said, taking another lunge at it. Slowly, slowly and very painfully I could feel it beginning to move. My hands were practically squeezing the arms of the dental chair out of existence. He gave a triumphant yell, holding his pincers up to the light to see what he had got. A sympathetic man, well aware of my pain, he was also shaking.

"Is that it?" I asked weakly.

"I wish it were," he answered. "I'm afraid that's just one root but at least it's a start. There are three other roots to come out yet. Do you think you can stand it?"

My spirits plummeted but I nodded. What would be the use of stopping now? He began to pull again. This time I didn't feel it quite so much. The removal of the one root had let the freezing in to a certain extent and it wasn't quite so painful. Otherwise, with what was to follow, I might not have been here to tell the tale. Every so often in his efforts to remove the remaining three roots, the dentist would rest from his labours, saying,

"Of course, if I'd known this was going to happen, I never would have started!"

This statement didn't cheer me greatly. Eventually there was another yell of triumph and another twisted root was held up for inspection.

"Only two to go now," he said, trying to sound light-hearted. I noticed he was sweating. Inwardly I groaned and not without reason. These last two roots would not budge!

"Looks like I'm gonna be beat after all," he said. "I'll have to take x-rays, I think, to see what's holding them back. How are you feeling? You've been marvellous – you really have!"

"Not bad," I lied but he must have seen the disappointment in my face.

"Wait a moment," he said, "just before I take these x-rays, I'll try one more thing. I'll use my little electric saw and separate the roots. If I'm successful that might help."

This new form of torture worked. Eventually he got both roots out separately. The reason for their obstinacy was revealed. Both were badly twisted and hooked.

"The worst tooth of its kind I ever did see," he said, adding again, "Of course if I had foreseen this, I would never have started!"

Battered but unbowed – I was jubilant.

"You're sure you'll be all right now?" the dentist asked anxiously. "Will you manage to drive home after your ordeal? How far have you got to go?"

"Not far," I assured him. "I'll manage thank you."

I tottered out to the car in a sort of daze. No need to tell the boys I had had a tough time. Children instinctively know these things. Richard especially, for all his tender years, was most solicitous.

"Just wait till you feel all right, Mummy, before you start driving," he said, sounding much older than his years and using the protective caring sort of voice his father would have used had he been present.

"Never mind the sweets today, we'll get them another day," he continued.

Tears of relief trickled down my cheeks, tears of love also for the kindness of people and the thoughtfulness of children that made everything worthwhile.

Chapter 20

Royal Whistlestop

"The Queen is coming to Sandyhills," Mandy and Susan burst in with this information one Saturday morning in July. I was taken by surprise.

"How exciting," I said. "When?"

"Next week," said Mandy, "and it's going to be great fun. There's to be a public holiday and everyone's arranging all sorts of things. It'll be like Stampede day all over again and – and, something more, we'll all have flags to wave . . ." Mandy babbled on.

"Who's the Queen?" Ronnie piped up.

"She's the Queen, silly," said Michael, while Richard, in the role of more knowledgeable elder brother, tried to give some sort of explanation.

The thoughts going through my head were strange. For Ronald and me the outside world had slipped into the background. We were too busy existing to take much notice or interest in what went on outside. We got no daily newspaper. Occasionally we listened to the radio and had heard that the Queen and Prince Philip were touring the Western Provinces but they covered such a huge area that we had not considered the possibility of them visiting Sandyhills.

On the radio there had been a certain amount of criticism about the Royal visit. Some Canadians, especially those belonging to ethnic groups other than British, were out and out opposed to it. They saw it as a kind of domination by Britain, albeit a slight one, and didn't want to be part of it. They felt totally Canadian and proud of it. Others, again, didn't mind. It made them feel different and their strongest desire was to be thought of as separate from the Americans. Opinions being so mixed

145

made some commentators on the radio sceptical about the whole affair. One had been very critical of the Queen when she had an unscheduled day off in some far northern place. She was sick.

"The poor Queen," I commented to Ronald, but it was a passing thought remote from the world I lived in.

And now, according to Mandy, she was coming to Sandyhills! So close, we might actually be able to go and see her. This altered the whole complexion of things. She became a flesh-and-blood person that stood for home in large letters. I had never thought of her in quite the same way before. When living at home in Scotland I had taken her for granted. Someone who was around from time to time. If she came to a local town to visit, as she did occasionally, I might or might not go to see her depending on what I was doing. It was much the same as our attitude had been to places like Hunting Tower Castle or Scone Palace that were within easy reach. We always meant to go and visit them but never actually did because we knew we could go there any time. But now the Queen was coming to Sandyhills – these acres of nowhere! I made an instant resolve to take the children to see her.

Nothing much was said by Jacobs about the Queen's visit but there were hints thrown out that, in spite of the work load, the men might get a day off as it was a public holiday. Adrian was over the moon. Always an optimist, he had all his day planned out and going to see the Queen was no part of it. He would get up at sunrise, take a quick cup of coffee, collect Gloria and set off along the gravel road for Edmonton – the big city! He got himself quite excited about it all.

On the Monday evening before the day of the Royal visit, just as the men knocked off for the night after a hard day shovelling grain, Jacobs said,

"We sure should be working on the far section across the railway tomorrow but do any of you guys want the day off to go and see the Queen?"

"I do," said Ronald. "Margaret very much wants to go and take the children and I'd like to go with her."

"And you Adrian?" asked Jacobs.

"I sure would like the day off," replied Adrian, "but I won't bother going to see the Queen. I've better things to do." Thereafter he made a few derogatory remarks about royalty in general, the Queen in particular. Jacobs' face froze.

"Right Adrian, that suits me fine. If you don't want to see the Queen you won't require a day off. First thing tomorrow morning, take the tractor and harrows to the furthermost end of the far section. . ." He then proceeded to give him detailed instructions of what he wanted him to do. Turning to Ronald he said,

"You can have the day off," with that he swung on his heels and marched off towards the house leaving Adrian gasping and for once speechless.

What the innocent Adrian hadn't realised was that Jacobs had a strong loyalist attitude to the British Royal family. Generations back his forbears were British. Therefore in a sense, he still felt British as well as being Canadian. However, whether one was for the British monarchy or against it, there was general excitement about the royal visit to Sandyhills. Here was a real excuse for celebration in this place where, year after year, nothing much happened.

The Queen and Prince Philip weren't to be long in Sandyhills. It was only a whistlestop. If we wanted to see them, we were told, we would have to go to the station. Ronald was pleased to learn that the train carrying the royal couple wasn't due in until the afternoon. He would be able to get a morning in bed. He had been feeling tired of late and and after a day shovelling grain the pain in his chest was bothering him. Ronald always made light of this pain saying that it was brought on by the long hours of work Jacobs insisted on. I wasn't altogether convinced by this explanation but as Ronald refused to do anything about it, I got into the habit of trying not to worry by living just one day at a time. At a much later date we were to discover that the pain was due to a heart defect that Ronald had had from birth. Something that had gone undetected in the pre-Canada medical.

On the morning of the Royal visit Ronald slept. I did my usual chores in the cabin and then stepped out into the warm sunshine to saw enough logs and carry enough water to last us a day or two. The saw was old and rather blunt and the trestle that held the wood had one leg shorter than the other which made it wobble a bit. In spite of that I enjoyed sawing logs. I liked the steady rhythm of the saw when it was going easily through a piece of wood. I liked the harsh rasping sound of it, seeing the sawdust fall like powder onto the ground, smelling the rich warm aroma of the bleeding wood. Also, a chipmunk would often make himself into a self-appointed overseer of my work, popping out now and again from amongst the dead wood and watching me with lively curiosity. But perhaps the greatest sense of satisfaction came from the sheer necessity of the job: you sawed up wood or did without cooked food and hot water.

The chore I didn't like was carrying water but here again it was stark necessity. The water had to be carried for some considerable distance (no handy pump at the door like we had at Redwoods).

One valuable thing I learned from these days in the prairie was the importance of water. Ever since that time I have never taken it for granted. In Scotland, as far back as I could remember, it had always come apparently endlessly out of a tap. At home it gurgled and leaped in all the burns, rushing down the hillside and joining that ever-widening river making for the sea. Until now I had never given water much thought. It had always come as dependably as daylight. Now I learned the art of conserving water. I had begun to realise that if we were to succeed – even more basically, survive, keep things from going badly wrong and perhaps putting the children in jeopardy – I had to learn to conserve energy and not become ill through overwork. That was of paramount importance. I worked out every conceivable way of saving water and thus reducing the strenuous task of carrying it so far. The water in the galvanised tub the children had been bathed in the night before was used for washing clothes next morning, paying careful attention to which clothes were washed first. Also, dishes were carefully wiped before being put into the water, thus it became possible to use the same water for dishes more than once.

On that royal morning by the time the chores were all done it was lunch time. Ronald was still asleep. I left him a little longer. The boys, however, were anxious to get away. Mandy and Susan

148

were already gone and they felt sure they would be missing something.

"When are we going – when are we going?" they kept asking me till I got annoyed with them. I gave them their lunch and then taking the galvanised boiler out on to the wooden veranda scrubbed each protesting boy in turn.

"What shirts would you like to wear?" I asked them knowing what the answer would be.

"The ones with the fishes on," they shouted in unison.

Ronald's sister had sent these and they were rich and bright. Back home I might have thought them a bit much but in this land of blue skies and glaring sun they looked good. I dared the boys to get dirty again in the time it took me to change Mahri-Louise into her best pink and white dress.

By the time we were ready, Ronald was ready too. He had risen of his own accord, dressed in his best clothes, had something to eat and looked much refreshed for his long sleep. We made our way through the cottonwoods to the old Chevrolet with its dusty green exterior and stone pitted windows. Ronald carried Mahri-Louise. I followed behind and thought how nice the boys looked skipping excitedly through the dappled shade of the trees.

Soon we were swinging

The tears were spilling down my cheeks. I was taken by surprise by the strength of my own emotion. This wouldn't have happened at home but here, in this alien place, she seemed part of all that I was part of, all that I remembered from the beginning.

along the gravel tracks, dust spinning out behind us, the car stirring up a haze that accompanied us wherever we went.

"Poor Adrian," Ronald said as we drove past a huge area of cultivated land across the railroad still to be worked.

"I'll bet he wishes he'd praised the Queen." I said as I looked through the dusty air and saw a tiny tractor-speck moving in the distance. It was moving along at some speed. Even from where I sat it looked angry.

When we got to Sandyhills the streets were deserted, although there were plenty signs of people having been there not long before. Stalls set up on the streets displaying sweets and popcorn had no one serving behind them. Braziers on the sidewalks were still smoking but in need of re-fuelling. The smell of newly baked pancakes seeped through the car window. A stray balloon or two drifted in the light breeze swirling away from us. There were flags everywhere but no people. It was as though some Pied Piper had come through the town and led everyone away.

Knowing where the people would be, we parked the car and hurried down to the station. We arrived just as the train pulled in and jostled our way through the flag-waving Canadians hoping to get a good view. We were fortunate to manage to wriggle our way to the track side due to Ronald's initiative, my determination to see the Queen, and the goodwill of the Canadian people who would go out of their way to accommodate children.

It is hard to describe the emotion I felt when I first saw her standing with her consort on the open-air platform at the back of the caboose. Here she was, waving to us all, a staunch, brave figure, smiling her familiar smile and looking a little more fragile than I had remembered. Prince Philip, standing protectively beside her was waving also. I stood, one toe touching the steel track that ran unbroken for thousands of miles eastward, and waved and waved. Ronald handed me Mahri-Louise in order to pick Ronnie up, placing him on his shoulder so that he could get a better view.

"There's the Queen, Ronnie. Now you know what a Queen looks like. Michael won't be able to call you silly again for not knowing."

Ronnie didn't seem to be impressed. He wanted a flag and a balloon.

By this time the tears were spilling uncontrollably down my cheeks into Mahri's shawl. I hoped no one would notice. I was taken by surprise by the strength of my own emotion. This wouldn't have happened at home but here, in this alien place, she seemed part of all that I was part of, all that I remembered from the beginning. She epitomised home. For one fleeting second I wished that Ronald and I and our family could get on that train with her and travel east over the long lonely terrain to the sea and beyond, back to our native shores.

The train didn't stop long. Slowly with a loud clanging from the bell it moved off cautiously. The people were milling round it, waving and cheering, almost preventing it from moving away.

"For goodness sake," Prince Philip shouted to one of the guards, "watch no one gets run over!"

But no one took any notice. They kept running after the train as it gathered speed. The cowboys, on restless horses, took off their stetsons and whooped, replaced them, took them off and whooped again, galloping after the train until we no longer saw them or the diminishing figure of the Queen.

Chapter 21

Stuck on the Highway

In Eastern Alberta in the fifties, if everyone went to town on a Saturday evening, everyone went to the lakes on a Sunday in the summer months. We also went from time to time. The nearest lake to us of any size was Bright Lake, a large expanse of sunlit water in an otherwise featureless plain. This was also a real family time out, mothers and daughters with picnic baskets, collapsible chairs and tables, colourful tablecloths – fathers and sons with fishing rods and axes for chopping firewood. We would leave the car in the shade of the sparse poplars and birches and make our way on to the shore to be among people and watch the fun in boats and waterskis. Once we travelled further to a Canadian salt lake – a small sea complete with waves, a beach and salty winds in the middle of a huge empty landmass.

We enjoyed these excursions but at the back of our minds was the knowledge that we would have to leave Jacobs' place before early winter set in. Jacobs hadn't said in so many words that he wouldn't require Ronald over the long winter months but every so often the information was implied. Although I had grown to like the place I knew we must leave. Jacobs was a man of dangerous moods. When would he break out next?

"I must find another job," Ronald said to me one day. "Something a bit closer to town. I don't think I really am the pioneering type. I would like, if possible, to break away from our railway sponsors and find a job for myself."

"Get the *Prairie Gazette*," I suggested. "I think the Jacobs buy it once a week. We could get one on Saturday when we go shopping."

The following Saturday we woke up to grey skies, which was most unusual. Actually we rather enjoyed it. It was pleasant for

152

once not to have the constant glare of the sun. All the contours of the earth were softer. Later in the morning the sun broke through and the skies became blue again, but not for long. Mandy and Susan came running over from the farmhouse to warn me about the weather.

"Dad says there is a storm brewing," said Mandy before Susan had time to get it out.

We saw it coming long before it arrived. Far away in the west, where we knew the ramparts of the Rocky Mountains made a barrier on the sky line, we could see a leaden blackness coming towards us. As it drew closer a wind rose and tumbleweed rolled across the prairie. Then thunder rumbled as powerful as the roaring of many lions and the sky was rent by electric blue threads illuminating the earth. I found it exciting to watch a storm coming for a hundred miles or more. Nothing that we could do would stop it. Eventually it reached us engulfing us in heavy rain that the soil soaked up in gratitude.

The storm had almost abated by the time we went on our weekly shopping excursion into Sandyhills. The streets and sidewalks were running with water. The sound of it was everywhere and people and shops had taken on a new kind of buoyancy. Everyone spoke to everyone else – for once they had a topic of conversation common to everyone – the rain! Now that the storm had passed it was just plain dull. It could have been a day back home in Scotland.

We were fortunate to get a *Prairie Gazette* as often they were sold out by the time we got into town. When we got home, after putting the children to bed and stowing away the groceries, we sat down by the black cook-stove to go through it looking for opportunities. The evening felt decidedly chill and for once damp. We were glad of the heat from the spurting and singing logs that smouldered to begin with, but burst into lively flames when they became sufficiently dry and warm. The kitchen smelt of poplar.

We found the column advertising jobs and avidly scanned its contents. It was longer than we expected and the advertisements were couched in a different language to that used back home – another English! Quite often we didn't really understand what they meant. Share cropping – what exactly did that term imply? In fact advertisements offered all sorts of schemes connected with farming that made us frighteningly aware of our lack of knowledge of the system by which farming worked in Canada. We had no blueprint for reading between the lines. There were very few straightforward jobs that would have been in any way suitable. Then almost at the end of the column –

FARM MANAGER WANTED
Doctor Knight wishes some capable
man in his early thirties to manage
his small and exclusive dairy herd
on an excellent farm near Edmonton.
Good wages. New immigrant would suit.
Good family house.

Ronald read it out several times. It seemed just right for us. As the address was supplied we decided to go and see it next day.

All the way to Edmonton! We had never been that far in the car before. What new townships would we see? – what new landmarks? – what new people? What adventures might befall us? I didn't expect the townships we passed to be up to much as the Jacob girls had often told us that Sandyhills was by far the best place on the road to Edmonton.

"The Jacobs will be wondering where we're off to," I said as we passed the farmhouse and saw Mandy lift up the edge of the lace curtain.

"Let them wonder," Ronald said and laughed.

The boys waved to Mandy from the back of the car and she waved back. They were looking forward to this new adventure and to coming back telling the girls all about it.

The landscape didn't change much mile after mile. It became a little less sandy perhaps, but otherwise the same plain contours lacking in distinctive features apart from the grain towers rising at intervals along the railroad like apostrophes on an almost empty page. However the crops and what scrub trees there were looked fresh after the rain. Some of the names of the small towns off the highway attracted my attention. Half way to Edmonton we came on a sign pointing to Pioneer.

"How do you think it would come by a name like that?" I asked Ronald

"Haven't the foggiest," he said. "But let's turn in and see if it has a shop open that sells Coke. I'm thirsty."

Pioneer wasn't unlike Sandyhills, only smaller and more rundown. It had a straggle of frame houses with paint peeling from the walls, a general store and flat-roofed post office which were closed, a rundown gas station, a bulky frame hotel. Down by the railroad the ubiquitous grain elevator gleamed in the sun and towered above the town, dwarfing another old frame house beside it and several derailed railway carriages that appeared to be inhabited. The township boasted only one main street and, as Mandy had warned me, was unpaved. In fact, today, after the deluge of rain, it was a sea of mud. Not far from the general store there was one other small shop. It appeared to be open.

"Stop here," I said. "I'll go and see if they've any Coke. You'd better not draw up too near the sidewalk, you might get stuck in the mud."

I opened the door of the car and gingerly stepped out into mud. I didn't want Ronald to get his shoes dirty when interviewing for a job but it wouldn't matter about mine. Soon I was standing on the wobbly wooden sidewalk and opening the screen door. It appeared to be a kind of coffee shop. A large counter ran the whole length of it where one or two men sat up on high stools drinking coffee out of greasy mugs. The whole interior looked none too clean. I was glad I was in for Coke in cans. I felt all eyes watching me but no one spoke. The only sounds were the buzzing of a fly and the whizz and splutter of a coffee machine. I asked for five cans of Coke. The man behind the counter reached up and brought them down from a shelf, wiping off the dust with his sleeve. He placed them on the counter baldly stating what I was due him. I paid him and as I turned to leave he spoke.

"You strangers around here?"

I said yes and made a hasty exit. I clutched the cans tightly to me, fearful they would fall in the mud and waded over to the car.

"Some place that was," I said to Ronald. "Let's get out of here and stop somewhere on the highway to drink."

Ronald started up the engine and tried to move off. I could feel the back wheels spinning in the mud. I had visions of having to return to the coffee shop and ask for assistance to push, but a few more attempts and we were off and thankfully lurched our way back on to the highway again.

"Satisfied?" asked Ronald.

I said nothing, but mentally decided not to ask again to see places with interesting names.

The advertised farm was more easily found than we had expected. It was quite close to Edmonton and on the east side, so that we didn't have to go through the city. That was a relief. When we actually pulled into the farm, however, our stomachs slumped. It was not what we had expected at all and certainly didn't live up to what was said in the advertisement.

"What a dump," said Ronald. I agreed.

"Just the same," I said, "if the owner seems a nice guy and the wages are good, don't refuse the job. This place is much more convenient for getting another job, perhaps in the city."

"Anyone that tells such lies in an advertisement can't be all that good," said Ronald sceptically.

I said no more and Ronald got out of the car to go and look for the owner. The children were getting restless and hungry. I got out the plastic container of sandwiches.

It was quite some time before Ronald returned. His face told me that all was not well.

"I'm definitely not coming here," he said after he got back into the driving seat.

"Did you see Doctor Knight?" I asked.

"No and I have no wish to," came the answer. "I was speaking to the man who is working here now. He showed me round. To begin with he really tried to be enthusiastic and then all of a sudden said, 'Look, you seem like a nice guy and I see you have a wife and young kids. Take my advice and don't come here. I shouldn't be telling you this. I'm not doing myself any good. The sooner Doc can get someone else, the sooner I can leave – I don't know why I don't just blow anyway. The Doc promises

156

you the earth and it's just a load of bullshit. The accommodation is terrible, the pay is worse and he leaves you to do everything singlehanded!' " We drove away in silence each vowing never to quite believe a Canadian advertisement again.

We headed for home as darkness was descending. Looking behind we saw the many lights of Edmonton twinkle invitingly, dancing and shimmering the way lights in the distance do in that curious half-light that heralds night. Brightest of all, on the eastern outskirts of the city a field of catalytic crackers rose in sparkling farewell. Close to, they had looked like tall steel Christmas trees decorated with fairylights. In front of us there were no lights, only the pale gold glow of acres of green-gold wheat almost ready for the combines.

As darkness came down in earnest the fields became dusty and indistinct. Soon the lights of the car probed into the empty darkness showing us little more than the gravel channels in front of the wheels. The car swung easily along, however, and to brighten our flagging spirits we started to sing. The boys joined in, humming when they weren't sure of the words. Even Mahri-Louise started to croon. We had travelled about thirty miles in this fashion when Ronald said,

"Am I imagining things or are these headlamps growing dimmer?"

I hadn't been paying much attention, but began to take more notice. It was quite true. The lights weren't very bright. As the car continued to eat up the miles their light became weaker and weaker. Ronald stopped the car and got out. He lifted up the bonnet but it was too dark to see anything and we didn't have a torch. Getting back into the car he said,

"We'll just keep going as long as there is any light left. Perhaps, if we're lucky, the moon will come up and we can drive home by moonlight. Now that Edmonton's well behind us there's no traffic to speak of.

Eventually the car lights went out altogether and we were forced to stop.

"I think the car battery must be discharging instead of charging. There is nothing I can do about it here," said Ronald.

The moon did eventually drift over the horizon but it was

157

only a golden crescent which lay like a slice of melon on a dark backcloth – beautiful but not enough light to see by. The road loomed darkly in front of us. We still had a long way to go. We reckoned we might be about half way home. Apart from the moon and a sprinkling of stars there was no light and no sign of any habitation.

"We'll just have to wait till some car passes," Ronald said.

We had been told that any driver on the road was helpful to another if they were stuck. A breakdown could happen to anyone and one might be many miles from help. In winter time, in the sub-zero temperatures of this far northern land it could be a matter of life and death.

"If we do have to wait till dawn," Ronald continued, " Jacobs isn't going to be too pleased. We have a busy day ahead of us."

"To pot with Jacobs!" I said, getting a bit ratty. "He'll just have to wait."

"Will we have to stay here all night," a boy's treble voice piped from the back seat. The question came from the ever wakeful Richard. The other two boys had fallen asleep. Mahri-Louise who had been sleeping in my arms for some time woke and started to cry. We explained to Richard what had happened. Usually willing to concede to any adventure, he didn't sound too happy. I managed to quieten Mahri-Louise and for a while all was still.

"What's that funny noise outside, Daddy?" Richard's voice piped up again.

Ronald rolled down the window. A thin cloud spun across the moon's bright crescent making it into a ghost of its former self. From the wilderness beyond the car that wild, mad, eerie howling that I had heard that first morning at Red Deer, once more took over the surrounding world, bringing my flesh out in goose pimples. Quickly Ronald shut the window.

"You know these big light-coloured dogs we see in Jacobs' fields sometimes? The ones that run away if they see you, but always stop and look over their shoulders at us before they disappear?" he said.

"You mean the coyotes?" said Richard, a little disparagingly telling us he didn't need all this kid-type explanation.

"Yes, the coyotes," Ronald confirmed. "That's the noise they make at night when they're calling to one another."

Oddly Ronald and I had hardly heard the howling of the coyotes since coming to Sandyhills, although there were plenty of them around. Richard had probably never heard the noise before. They certainly were in good voice tonight. Perhaps all the rain had something to do with it, relieving parched throats.

Richard didn't seem entirely convinced that such ordinary harmless-looking dogs as the coyotes he had seen could make so fearsome a sound. Was Daddy telling tales? Lying to keep something from him so that he wouldn't be frightened? In the back seat Michael stirred.

"Are we home?" he asked in a sleepy voice.

"No we're not," said Richard before I had time to say anything, "we're stuck and outside there's . . .

"Richard be quiet!" I said breaking in before he said any more. I dreaded the reactions of Michael to the weird howlings beyond the car window.

"Let's sing a song – *It's a long way to Tipperary,*" I began; Ronald, Richard and Michael's sleepy voice joined in. After the song had petered out, I said, "I know what – I'll tell you a story, then after that, we'll sing more songs." I made up a fantastic tale about some daylight event to keep them all from noticing the night. Then we had more songs and a story from Ronald and more songs. Eventually, even Richard fell asleep.

The night now became very quiet, even the coyotes were silent. I fell into a short series of cat naps with one ear always alert, listening for the hoped for sound of an approaching motor. It must have been in the small hours of the morning when I first heard it in one of my wakeful periods.

Ronald wound down his window. Unmistakably we could hear the sweet drone of a motor approaching – music to our ears. Simultaneously we looked round and saw through the rear window, two beams of light, dusty and dim at first, then brighter and brighter. Suddenly the noise and the lights were upon us. A car drew up with a squeal of brakes, throwing a cloud of gravel around us. A young, broadshouldered man jumped energetically out of the driver's seat.

"You folks sure look stuck!" he said through Ronald's open window. "Where you making for?"

"Sandyhills and we are!" Ronald barely had time to explain the situation before the young man said,

"Soon fix that!" and had opened the boot of his car bringing out a stout rope. Then with quick deft movements he got back into his car drawing it immediately in front of our one. He jumped out again to tie our front bumper to his back one and we were off at speed, swinging along the gravel ruts. It was only then we noticed that the car we were so dangerously following was filled with young men in soldier's uniform. Occasionally a window would open, we would hear a wild whoop and a beer can would be flung out the window.

They're all drunk," I said. " Keep on the brakes, try to slow things down a little! What can we do?"

"There's nothing we can do!" Ronald replied, "other than keep singing and trust to luck!"

And that is exactly what we did. We sang all the way home on that mad wild drive through the dark night, gravel flying around us.

We arrived in Sandyhills as dawn broke – a wonderful red wash of light covering the sky, deepening in intensity until an enormous sun appeared over the far rim of the horizon. We were still alive!

Almost as suddenly as the soldiers had stopped for us, they drew up when we entered the empty streets of Sandyhills. The young driver slid from his seat and undid the tow rope.

"Great ride!" he said. "Great morning! – see you around, folks!" and they were off again in the direction of the army camp. He had given us no time to thank him or offer him payment which was perhaps just as well. Ronald and I were so stunned with relief that I wondered afterwards if any words would have come.

Chapter 22

Joe's Little Acre

The visit to the Knight farm was the last of our Sunday excursions. After that it was harvest time. Jacobs, Ronald and Adrian took it in shifts to drive the combine working day and night in this land of short growing seasons and long winters. The prairies were pure gold now and the minds of men centred on cutting that gold down and extracting the seeds from the full bright ears of grain.

I saw little of Ronald in these busy harvest days and nights and when I did, he was usually too tired to say much. The days were bright and warm but we knew winter was approaching fast. We had been warned over and over again of its early arrival. However, it was hard to believe during these golden days that it would ever come.

I knew we would be leaving Jacobs' place although nothing had been said. In spare moments I cleaned windows until they shone and scrubbed floors till they came up white. I wanted to leave the house as clean as possible.

It wasn't until early in September and the harvest was almost over that Jacobs mentioned it to Ronald.

"Well, what are you folks figuring on doing this winter? The house you're in ain't just suitable for winter living on account of it havin' bin moved around. I guess it could be fixed up but if you do stop over I can only offer you half pay."

Ronald thanked him for his offer and said that we would probably be moving on. That night he wrote a letter to our railway sponsors giving them our position and saying we found it hard enough living on a full wage let alone one cut in half for the winter months, and could they possibly find us another job?

We got a quick reply telling us to pack up all our possessions and be at their office in Edmonton at 10am sharp on the 9th of September, where a dairy farmer would be waiting to interview Ronald. It didn't give us much time. Ronald told Jacobs at the first opportunity. Jacobs wasn't too pleased at the suddenness of it all.

"You'll sure need to work up till the last minute," he said. "There's a lot needin' doin around here yet!"

Ronald promised Jacobs to work until the 8th telling him that he would need to go to Edmonton a day early to be in time for the appointment.

Jacobs gave an annoyed grunt but made no further comment and so it was that Ronald was kept busy until 10pm on the 7th of September.

I had been hard at work all week and by the 8th all our possessions were ready for Ronald to pack into the car. We wanted if possible to take all that we had with us, leaving only the packing cases behind. Everything, somehow, would have to be squeezed into the Chevrolet. Ronald had told me to leave this to him, priding himself on being an excellent packer, a past master at getting a lot into a little space!

On the 8th of September we woke to overcast skies. The boys were up before us, excited about the move to the city and eager to help their Dad pack the car. Ronnie and Michael were apt to get in the way but Richard was a real help running with things from the house. As Ronald loaded the Chevrolet it grew darker and darker and then, to our surprise, the first snow of winter began to fall, huge flakes drifting calmly down. The land seemed to accept them as a natural matter of course.

Although too busy to think of anything but the immediate job, my heart was as heavy as the morning skies. I knew we must go but already I had put down tentative roots in this place. I liked this 'living with the elements'. I felt I had really got to know the summer face of Canada as it had always been. I felt part of it, one with the bluebirds and the brown-eyed-susans. It would have been interesting to stay and help fix up the house to make it habitable for winter. For all our grumbles about Jacobs' faults including his dangerous moods, he was an able, fair and in many ways, helpful man. With the inability to sell grain we knew money would be tight for them but we just couldn't afford to feed the children on the money they offered us. We had to move on.

The afternoon was half over before we got everything packed into the car and were ready to go. I wanted to get away at least before the girls got back from school. They had been in the previous evening saying their goodbyes and Mandy, in particular, was upset. Large tears appeared in her ardent blue eyes.

"Don't cry Mandy!" Richard said. "We'll be back to see you soon."

Adrian had been round to visit us too and we promised to write to him as soon as we settled somewhere giving him our address. He promised to pay us a visit if we weren't too far away.

As it was, we didn't get away as soon as we hoped we would and the whole family came to see us off. Adrian and Elmer were there too as they were both near at hand, it being too bad a day for working further afield. Everyone marvelled at how much Ronald had managed to pack in the car. The three boys were perched high up in the back seat on top of everything like three little sparrows. Betty Jacobs, kind as ever, had made us sandwiches for the journey. Nothing much was said but I noticed that her eyes were as moist as my own.

At last the emotional moment was over and we were off. The snow had stopped falling, much to our relief, but the gravel road looked different with its new white covering. Ronald drove more slowly than usual, not knowing what effect snow might have in these deep ruts. Also the car was well loaded down and we didn't want to break any springs. I sat back with Mahri-Louise in my arms and breathed a sigh of relief. At last we were on our way with the work all done.

It began to snow again. We drove on into its confusing whiteness. It began to worry Ronald and me who, up until then, had had no time to worry about the weather. Fortunately after a while it stopped, but by now the road in front of us and the prairies around us were taken over by darkness. It was a strange experience, this steady moving on into the night, the old Chevrolet holding all the paraphernalia we possessed and our dearest treasures, the children, squabbling in the back, the baby in my arms. The boys were not worrying at all. They were so sure father and mother knew where they were going and would shortly find another nest. But did we? Would we?

For what seemed a long time we went on through the night with no lights of human habitation visible anywhere. Yet all the time I felt a light I could not see but knew awaited us at the other end. I started to sing and soon everyone was joining in. One by one the children fell asleep and to the soothing steady drone of the engine, the swaying motion of the tin-can body that held together all that we had, I felt myself nodding off also.

It was midnight when we reached the outskirts of Edmonton. For some time the lights of the city had come closer and closer as if to say 'Welcome to the city of dreams'

I was sceptical of finding anywhere at this late hour but Ronald appeared more confident. As it turned out, it seemed as if he drove without a compass but we were dead on course. We came to a collection of cabins on the edge of the highway – half a dozen at least. They stood, attractive shadows, each with its own pool of light radiating from a lamp above the door. Across the white gate leading into this small complex spanned a sign which said in large easily read letters –

WELCOME TO JOE'S LITTLE ACRE

After midnight it may have been, but the place didn't look dead. We saw a young couple slip from a car and open one of the cabin doors. We turned in through the gateway and were confronted by a cabin somewhat larger than the others. Over the door it said simply 'JOE' and further down 'PLEASE RING' – an arrow pointing to a bell. Ronald drew the car to a halt and stepped out. Before he had time to reach the bell the door was opened by a tall man with a rugged face sporting a generous mouth. I liked his appearance. He had an open face, a kind face.

"You guys are sure late on the road," he said but he didn't sound surprised. "Come a long way?"

"Over a hundred miles, east," Ronald said adding, "Any possibility of getting a cabin for the night?"

"Sure, sure just wait a moment until I get my keys."

Soon he was striding in front of us guiding us along the rough track that led to the furthest-away cabin. Joe slipped the key in the lock and the door opened easily.

"It's all yours, folks," he said and left us to it.

He didn't even ask for money in advance which gave us a warm glow inside. Because we had no credit rating, we had come to expect to have to pay for things when or before we got them. Joe didn't know us. We had driven in out of the night. In this sort of situation, who knows, we could have kipped down for a few hours and then made off in the early hours of the morning to be in another state before anyone could catch up with us – British Columbia, Saskatchewan – another country even – America! I remarked on the fact to Ronald.

"Yes it's good isn't it," he said.

We didn't need to say any more, knowing exactly how each other felt.

The boys, perched in the back of the car, uncomfortable as it was, were still fast asleep. They had wakened momentarily when we stopped at Joe's house but had fallen asleep again. I got out of the car. I felt stiff with sitting in a cramped position for so long. Household goods were all packed round my legs. Ronald held out his arms to take the sleeping baby.

Together we explored the little house and, like two children, were enchanted. It was small but everything we could possibly need was there – the luxury of a flushing toilet, a shower, electric cooker, vacuum sweeper for the floor – two bunk beds in one small bedroom, one double bed for us next door. There was even a cot lying against one wall ready to assemble should it be required. Like children going to a new house or hotel we tried everything, especially the plumbing. The taps actually ran with hot and cold water. The shower splashed down like warm summer rain. The toilet flushed with a noisy rush, music to our deprived ears. The two electric rings on the cooker went on with the simple turn of a switch. Everything was bright and clean. The floors were polished. Here and there rugs lay scattered around to give a splash of colour to the chalet. We didn't really notice that the walls were thin, the paint cheap, what furniture there was made of matchwood, the gilt on the taps so thin that

165

it would roll off before long. Ever since that exploration in the small hours of an Albertan morning I have been able to understand the lure of pictures of ideal homes in glossy magazines. To those who have had nothing, they must seem like some sort of heaven and no amount of telling them that it might be a false one would be likely to convince otherwise.

After we had examined everything Ronald said,

"I think we should carry the boys in and put them straight into their bunks just as they are. I'm sure they'll sleep."

For once Ronald was wrong. His plan might have worked had it not been for Richard. As soon as we carried him into the chalet he was wide awake.

"Where are we? he asked.

"Joe's Little Acre on the outskirts of Edmonton," Ronald replied.

Richard accepted this without further question and began running about the house. He flushed the toilet, turned on the taps, tried the shower. We couldn't say much. We had done the same ourselves. Ronnie and Michael might have gone straight to sleep again had Richard let them but before long they were running around trying everything also. Richard's eyes were huge with excitement. For once Ronnie's were even bigger and rounder. Six months was a long time in the life of a two year old – a quarter of his life. He probably wouldn't remember what life had been like in Scotland. While the children were exploring I fed and changed Mahri-Louise and helped Ronald assemble the cot. Suddenly I felt thirsty.

"How about a cup of coffee?" I asked.

"Good idea!" said Ronald and plugged in the electric kettle. I took down the mugs from a neat row of hooks. Ronald brought the basket containing coffee, sugar, milk and orange juice and Betty Jacobs' remaining sandwiches in from the car. It was all so easy, no water to pump or carry, no logs to saw, no old black stove to coax into burning.

After this meagre feast in the middle of the night, everyone was ready for bed. The boys suddenly became anxious to try out the bunks, squabbling over who would sleep in which bunk, everyone wanting a top one.

From nowhere in particular words came into my head – old words learned a long time ago.

> The bairnies cuddle doon at nicht
> Wi' muckle faucht and din.

We made no delay either in slipping into the most comfortable bed we had slept in since coming to Canada. There we slept the sleep of the very tired, the reassured and the hopeful.

Chapter 23

A Day of Change

Next morning Ronald had to be at our sponsor's office at ten o'clock sharp. It might take us some time to get into the centre of town, find the right address and get somewhere to park.

As soon as light filtered into the cabin the boys were up and came running through to the the kitchen-cum-livingroom where I was feeding Mahri.

"Mummy, look out the window," they said in unison, "there's swings, a chute and a sandpit. Can we go out and play?"

I peered out the window. I had to sound strict with the boys – there wouldn't be much time.

"If you have a shower, get dressed quickly and have your breakfast there may be time to go out for a little while, but you'll have to be quick. We must be away by nine."

This worked wonders. Without the incentive of getting outside they might have spent hours in the shower. Ronald made the breakfast while I got dressed. Fortunately we had brought bacon, bread and cereal with us. At nine we were ready to go.

It was hard dragging the boys away from the small playground. They would have been quite happy to stay there all day.

We stopped at Joe's cabin to hand in the key and pay the night's lodgings. We were surprised it cost so much, although later we learned how cheap it was in comparison with the average motel prices. Joe was chatty and seemed more curious about us than most Canadians had been. He asked us, directly, where we had come from, where we were bound for and what we intended doing. Equally directly, Ronald told him. He had taken a liking to the man and Joe being a complete stranger, there could be nothing to lose by telling him our position – no reason for keeping anything back. It turned out a good idea to tell him. Joe immediately put himself about to help us, asking us to hold on a minute while he looked for a street map of Edmonton. He brought one from his house and opened it up on the bonnet of the car. Ronald clambered out to study it. Joe showed him how best to get to the centre of the city and where to park to be closest to his destination. He also gave us important do's and don'ts. If we disobeyed the strict traffic laws, he told us, we would soon be accosted by police. We thanked Joe for his information and Ronald started up the engine once more. As a parting gesture, just as we were moving off, Joe shoved the map through Ronald's open window.

"Here, you folks," he said, "take this. Don't want anything for it and if things don't go according to plan you'll sure be welcome back here."

We were sad to leave in such a hurry. With our usual confidence that everything would be all right, we thought it highly unlikely that we would see Joe or his 'Little Acre' again. The boys all waved and we were off.

And so began what was to become one of the most trying days of my life. If it was bad for me and the boys, it was equally bad for Ronald though in a different way. The first difficulty was driving to our destination. In spite of Joe's helpful advice and good directions, Ronald found problems. It seemed a long time since we had driven along busy roads. Entering the city we were surprised to find just how rustic we had become. Also the road systems here were more advanced than back home. We had never remotely heard, in these days, of spaghetti junctions. Here at the entrance to this far northern city, one sprouted its tubular strands. How Ronald coped I do not know. I could not have coped with these roads, at that time, without getting in a panic.

The city of Edmonton, seen from the outskirts, appeared rather plain. We crossed the High Level Bridge and looked down into a chalk-coloured river. The streets of Edmonton were well organised, everything marked off in blocks, the streets running one way, the avenues another; nothing haphazard like back home. Even so, for us newcomers, finding our way was difficult. Ronald did eventually find the parking lot Joe had advised us to use. Ronald looked at his watch and noticed that already he was five minutes late for his appointment.

"Blast!" he said," knowing the rate at which Canadians do things. I hope the man hasn't come and gone," and with those few words dashed off. The day was, as usual, sunny with no vestige of yesterday's snow anywhere. The boys, perched high on the back seat, had managed to twist round on their knees to peer out the thin strip of back window and watch all the cars coming in and out of the parking lot. This kept them amused for ages. After the first hour, however, they began to get bored and wanted to get out. As this was a busy parking lot I couldn't let them out on their own. If I had gone with them I would have had to carry Mahri-Louise as her fold-down pram was inaccessible. I couldn't leave her in the car not knowing what dangers might lurk in a strange city. If I took her my hands would be full and the cooped-up boys might take off in all directions as they had done in Montreal station. We played 'I Spy' for a while, but Ronnie was really too young to play this game and began to be naughty. Then I made up a story about three little boys who got lost. This interested them for a while until they began to fight over something trivial. At long last Ronald appeared. He had been gone two hours.

"Well?" I questioned eagerly as he got into the car, "where are we going to this time?"

"We're not!" replied Ronald, "or at least, not yet!"

"What do you mean," I said, a sudden knot of worry numbing my brain.

"Our so-called new employer hasn't showed up yet. They could give me very little helpful information as to when he would arrive. I would still be sitting there but I explained to them about you and the children jammed into the car. Fat lot they care, but they did let me out for a while, asking me to come back in an hour, saying he would almost sure to have appeared by that time."

"He'll probably come all right," I said, worry subsiding. "In the meantime perhaps we could take the boys to stretch their legs. They've been good but are getting restless." I tried not to grumble because I knew it was hard enough for Ronald having to hang around and wait, without telling him it was beginning to be hell in the car.

"Please Daddy take us out, please!" came an excited chorus from the back.

The car was hot. Because of this, Mahri-Louise, usually a docile baby, was fractious. The walk in the fresh air would do her good. Perhaps being held in my arms would rock her to sleep.

After being cooped up the walk down Edmonton's broad main street was heaven. There weren't all that many people walking about and those that were seemed in a hurry. There were a few children about with their mothers. One woman passed us wheeling a pram. It looked odd. It had a round hood which reminded me of a covered wagon. Another woman passed quickly carrying her baby completely wrapped in a shawl. Even the baby's face was covered. I got the impression that the mother thought it was dangerous to have a baby exposed to the air.

The boys, glad to be out, danced and skipped down the wide-paved sidewalk. They were perfectly controllable with Ronald about. We bought some books for them in a drugstore where we also had a snack – wieners in long soft rolls dripping with onions and tomato sauce, also Coke for the boys, coffee for Ronald and me. When we got back Ronald noticed an empty space in the shade and shifted the car. He looked at his watch. It was time to go again.

"Perhaps I won't be long this time," he said. "Surely the farmer will be there by now."

The boys all waved to Dad out the back window then turned with interest to the books we had bought.

The minutes, the hours dragged on. The sun shifted round to stream into the car once more and soon we were all too hot again, even with all the windows open. I would have shifted the car but there were no shady spaces vacant. Mahri-Louise was crying non-stop now. At last I saw Ronald hurrying towards us. Relief flooded through me. To begin with I didn't notice the serious expression on his face.

"He hasn't come yet," he said, but still they say he won't be long. They've let me out for a wee while, at my insistence. They

171

just don't seem to understand the position we're in!"

Again I didn't tell him just how difficult things were becoming but I couldn't altogether hide it. He could see the situation for himself, hear the din they were all making. We all got out of the car for a minute or two and then Ronald dashed off to get cans of Seven-up and packets of popcorn. He left saying very little this time. The boys enjoyed the picnic in the car and afterwards, much to my relief, fell asleep. Mahri-Louise followed suit after a feed and an awkward change of nappies. I, too, nodded off. Gradually the hot sticky afternoon wore on.

It was after four when Ronald came back the next time. I could see anger in his eyes, also new resolution.

"He hasn't showed up yet!" he said. "Come back at six, they say, don't leave it longer than that."

"You could drive us back to Joe's Little Acre," I said, "and come back on your own at six . . ." my words trailed away. Ronald wasn't listening. Something had changed in the atmosphere. I could feel it in my bones.

"That's me finished with the sponsors," he said in a voice that brooked no contradiction. "I didn't come to Canada with no thought other than farming anyway. I want to try something else and now's the time."

"Did you tell them that?" I asked.

"No," he replied, "and I don't intend to."

I said no more accepting the fact that, once again, life for us was going to change dramatically.

"We'll go back to Joe's Little Acre," Ronald said. "Start again tomorrow."

172

Chapter 24

Looking for a Home

Joe didn't seem all that surprised to see us when we arrived back on his doorstep.

"Thought you folks might be back," he said handing us the key, "kept your cabin for you!"

By way of explanation Ronald told him of our difficult day and how, quite suddenly, something had snapped in him and he made up his mind to forget about the sponsors. Joe made little comment about this, not saying whether he thought it a wise move or a foolish mistake. He probably saw Ronald had made up his mind anyway, and anything he said would be ignored. Ronald went on to tell him that we intended renting a house in Edmonton and asked how to go about it.

"It's sure not difficult," he said. "A lot of them cost a bit. Get an Edmonton paper and you'll find them listed there."

We were relieved to hear this. Back home it could be quite difficult getting accommodation. Rules and regulations were becoming so strict that landlords were inclined to sell off their property rather than rent it. Joe told us that there were very few rules here and consequently all sorts of places for rent, even rooms in houses. Joe, as before, was very practical and helpful. He told us where to get the newspaper that listed them and which supermarket sold the best and cheapest food.

The boys were delighted to be back in Joe's Little Acre and the moment they were allowed to escape from the car made for the swings. Ronald, also without delay, went to get a carry-out meal for us all, some essential supplies from the supermarket Joe had recommended, and a newspaper from the nearby drugstore.

That evening after the boys were fast asleep in their bunks

and Mahri-Louise in her cot, Ronald and I studied the long columns of accommodation for rent. We carefully marked those that looked most suitable.

"I'll go and see them tomorrow," said Ronald. "No need for you and the children to come with me. If I find something that I think will do, I'll come and take you to see if you like it."

Ronald was later than I expected in arriving home the following day. When he left in the morning he assured me he would be home by teatime and I had made a particularly nice meal for him. When he did eventually turn up he looked tired and dejected. Anxiously I asked him how his day had gone.

"Not too well," he admitted. "Every house or flat has some snag or other. I wasn't being at all fussy but the main snag is price. They all seem very expensive – more than we can afford! I've only come up with one that might do. I'll take you to see it tomorrow – it's not much, but at least it's within our price range. It's a big old house down by the river, one of the first houses built in Edmonton probably. The worst thing about it is that the owner, an old man, lives in it also. He has two rooms of his own partitioned with a piece of sacking over his door. . ."

I had been ready to agree to almost anything but inwardly I stiffened when he mentioned the old owner occupier. I didn't like the sound of that at all. I could see however that Ronald was dispirited and knew that the money we had brought from Scotland was running out. I promised I would look at the house.

It was worse than I expected. I knew, as soon as I saw it, that I wasn't going to live there. It was old and hadn't stood the test of time all that well. The paint, once white, was very dingy and peeling off in places. There were several shingles missing from the roof but worse than that, it stood all by itself in a sort of muddy swamp down by an uninteresting stretch of river. Here and there, town garbage littered the mud.

Try as I could, I found it hard even to imagine Red Indians in their canoes paddling past on the chalk-coloured water. I'd read somewhere that they had used this river in the old days, before there were roads or the railway. Once it had been the main highway of commerce at the time when the Hudson Bay Company had set up their bare outposts at intervals along its sandy flats. Today what made the landscape even bleaker was that there were no trees and very little greenery. If there ever had been trees they were all gone now and even with the sun lighting the whole area it was gloomy and depressing.

The old man showed us over the house. I hardly looked at the rooms at all. In my mind's eye all that I saw was the mud and this man watching us from behind the sacking door and shuddered!

"What do you think?" said Ronald, when we returned to the car.

"Not unless there is nowhere else in the whole of Edmonton," I said.

At a later date when telling friends of some of our difficulties, they would ask me, "Did all these problems not put a great strain on your marriage?"

At the time I never thought about it but looking back I'm sure it did the opposite, it strengthened us. In the position we were in there was no room for disagreement. The conflict must not be between us but with the difficult and dangerous outside world. There were minor squabbles and disagreements but I don't remember them and on this particular morning I could see Ronald was almost at the end of his endurance while I was, by now, feeling well-rested with a renewed confidence and vigour. There came a sudden resolve inside me and before he could speak I continued.

"Tomorrow we'll start again. This time I'll come with you and we'll scour the whole of Edmonton. We'll come up with something, you'll see!"

We had a good night's sleep and after breakfast, set out with restored hope, prepared to spend the whole day looking at houses and flats. Ronald was beginning to get used to driving in a Canadian town.

"It's quite easy really," he said, "once you get the hang of it."

That morning we travelled far and wide, up and down its avenues and streets. The problems were as Ronald had told me – suitable houses or flats were too expensive for our now meagre purse, cheaper accommodation were rooms that shared a kitchen and perhaps a bathroom, or compact but stuffy small basement flats smelling faintly of gas.

"One more before we take the kids for lunch," I said to Ronald.

We were on our way back to Joe's Little Acre when we turned up a suburban avenue. It wasn't the complete house that was to let here, just the basement flat. The advertisement said that it had three bedrooms, a living room, a kitchen and a bathroom. It sounded big enough. Joe, however, had warned us about basement flats.

"Folks say that they're none too healthy on account of them being down under and adjacent to the heating system, which is usually a boiler using natural gas. Just the same," he continued, "young couples sure go for them because they're cheap. Often they don't stay long. People in Alberta are always moving on."

The moment we turned into its wide street I liked it. It gave me a good feeling. I knew at once I wanted to live there. The houses in the avenue were all different in shape and size. Many of them were attractive. Some were built completely of wood, left in the simple beauty of its natural graining and highlighted with a coat of varnish. Others were painted in sparkling white or bright clear colours that gleamed in the brilliant sunshine. Metallic cars were dotted here and there to add to the brightness. The houses had been constructed long enough on the cleared land to allow some trees to grow to a reasonable height. These were mostly quick-growing birches and poplars. The gardens themselves were uninspiring. Mostly areas of burnt-up grass which ran down to the sidewalk, often without the impediment of fences.

There were young children about, playing with tricycles and buggy-type doll's prams, small replicas of the one I had seen a few days before in the streets of Edmonton. I sensed freedom for children in these communal gardens. There were garden patches at the back also which we only caught glimpses of on our first visit to 147 Avenue but which we came to know more about. The more provident of the owners watered them well and grew vegetables that shot up like beanstalks in the very short growing season.

176

In winter these same back gardens were converted into ice rinks, layer after layer of water being smoothly sprayed on until a gleaming patch of ice grew hard and compact. There the older children, clad in quilted cotton anoraks, spent hours skating and playing fierce games of ice hockey.

Today, ice rinks were far from our thoughts. We looked along the row of houses on either side. One house, about half way along the row, stood out above the rest. It was built of wood and had recently been painted white. Here and there touches of black were visible. Something about the simplicity of its lines and the way it towered above the other houses reminded me of a church. This house as it turned out was the one we were looking for. When we reached it the door down to the basement was open. Tentatively we went down a few steps. At the bottom, beside a large gas boiler, a woman was on her hands and knees scrubbing the floor.

"Excuse me," Ronald said, "is this the basement flat advertised for rent?"

The woman didn't get up immediately but sat back on her haunches looking at us from the depth of her dark brown eyes. Her glance was quick but thorough. I felt sure she already knew all about us.

"Yes," she said simply.

"Could we see through it please," I asked.

Obligingly she showed us all the rooms. It was a nice little flat with everything in it we could possibly want. It was clean and warm and the price was reasonable. I looked at Ronald.

"What do you think?" I asked.

"If you like it," he said.

I turned to the landlady.

"We'll take it," I said, "although I must warn you we have quite a big family." I was genuinely worried that this might be a stumbling block as it would have been at home.

"How many?" she asked.

"Four," I confessed.

"I have eight," she replied. Without anything more being said the bargain was completed. She told us we could move in next day.

Chapter 25

Looking for a Job

Once we got settled into our new home in Edmonton, I allowed the boys out to play on the patch of plain grass in front of the house. The days were beginning to get cold now but I wrapped them up well. At first I was worried that they would run on the road but fortunately not many cars passed in the daytime. I noticed that other children were allowed to play quite freely.

One day I questioned our landlady about the gardens.

"Most people sure don't bother with gardens too much," she said. "I guess it's because we're all too busy with other things. It's difficult to have a nice garden. Flowers are the darndest thing to grow because of the lack of water. You just about never see American beauty roses here although I suppose they would grow if someone paid enough attention to them. Anyway, those who do work in their gardens tend to concentrate on vegetables – something useful – good for the kids. Children are looked on as a useful crop in Alberta. We need people."

One afternoon several days after moving into the basement flat, a knock came at the door. I opened it to find a woman about my own age standing there with a large bundle of clothes in her arms.

"I see you have ze little childer," she said in a strong German accent, "Zees clothes no longer feet my leetle ones, please to have them."

Before I had time to thank her, she had gone. The rest of the afternoon was spent by the boys trying on all the things she had brought and quarrelling over who would get what. There were some useful garments for the baby also and as Mahri-Louise was growing fast, new clothes were essential. Seeing the children in all their new togs I said to Ronald,

"They're beginning to look like real little Canadians now aren't they?" Ronald agreed.

The gift from the German woman gave us a new surge of hope that everything was going to be all right. We needed this boost. Things weren't going well in the business of job hunting.

"There just isn't anything," Ronald had said the evening before after a third day's unsuccessful hunting. "For all the jobs that are advertised, when you look into them, there is hardly a genuine offer amongst them. There's one type of job I would like to try. There are quite a few vacancies, but anyone I happen to mention it to says it is far too risky. You get payed on a commission basis only."

"What sort of job?" I asked although I felt I already knew. I had seen Ronald linger over some ads longer than others.

"Real Estate," he answered, "the buying and selling of houses and land."

For once I was silent not knowing quite what to say – one half of me worried about the welfare of the children, the other wanted to let Ronald do what he wished. After all, that was our main reason for coming to Canada. For the time being I hedged the issue.

"Do you remember brother-in-law Bill gave us the address of a lady in Edmonton? He said to be sure to go and see her. He told us what a helpful person she was. Perhaps she would be able to give us advice. I must have her name and address somewhere. I'll have a look."

Eventually I unearthed her address and Ronald said he would pay her a call the next day. He came back more dejected than ever.

"Did you see Mrs Neville?" I asked.

"She's a pleasant person," he said, "but Bill, when he told us about her, had forgotten about the passage of years. She's old now and all she wants is peace. She doesn't want strangers invading her privacy, although she was quite glad to see me and hear news of Bill."

"Did you ask her for her advice on jobs?"

"Yes, but she wasn't very helpful and had no real suggestions. She heard it was very difficult to get a job of any kind in the city.

She also said not to touch Real Estate with a bargepole, or words to that effect!" Ronald gave a big sigh, "I think I'll have the weekend off. Try again next week."

Monday came and the job hunting started again. Ronald came home in the middle of the afternoon looking a bit brighter.

"I've come up with something," he said.

"A job in a grain mill – pretty low wages but perhaps we could just manage on them. It's going to be very hard physical work, though, a lot of lifting of heavy bags."

All of a sudden something clicked inside me. I'd made up my mind and I took the initiative. It wasn't the low wages that prompted me. We probably would have managed on what was offered – it was the mention of hard work and long hours that put me against it. I knew that Ronald wasn't really able for it. He still complained of that nagging pain in his chest and sometimes he looked very tired.

"You're not taking it," I said full of new resolution. "I don't honestly think you are able to take that kind of work until you have had a good rest. Anyway, what did we come to Canada for but to take risks although not with your health. Try the job you want to do – try Real Estate!"

With this new determined backing, Ronald took up the newspaper again. Turning to the relevant page he went through the various adverts. There was one in particular he had had his eye on all week.

EMPIRE REAL ESTATE
Wanted: a young aggressive man
to take on the buying and selling of property
outside the boundaries of Edmonton.
Huge profits possible
for the right man.

I glanced at the clock. It was three thirty.

"There's time yet," I said, "before the offices close. Go and see what they have to offer."

Ronald changed into the suit that he hadn't worn since landing in Canada and ran up the knot in his silk tie.

He arrived back about an hour later.

"I've got the job," he announced. "I think I'll like it. The manager is twenty nine, a few years younger than myself. I took an immediate liking to him. He's full of wild dreams, but practical too. My job will be to take on all the buying and selling for the firm, outside the boundaries of Edmonton. There's quite a variety of land and houses to sell. The manager told me I'll have a lot to learn. Acreages will be my bread and butter. Acreages are plots of land outwith the city limits with planning permission to build a house or houses. People in Edmonton who get fed up with city life buy them to build the house of their dreams. Also there are lakeside lots. These are small portions of land round a lakeside that people buy to erect their own summer cabins. Everything I do is on a commission basis. There will be no money until I have actually bought and sold something, but the commission is good and they would consider lending me something until I get started.

Ronald looked so happy that I suppressed any anxiety I had. I decided once again to live for the day only, worry about immediate problems and not to think too much about tomorrow. Who knew what might happen in this bright new land?

Chapter 26

Voice from the Ukraine

Our basement flat was roomy. It had three bedrooms – a living area with cook-stove and sink and it had a bathroom. It was half underground but the wide windows on the top half of the walls let in plenty of light and all the rooms were warm. If there was a bit of fug about we didn't complain because the house was superior to anything we had had in Canada so far. Immediately outside the livingroom door stood a huge natural gas burner which heated all three stories of the house. There was a large washing machine adjacent to the burner which I had permission to use – a great boon. The house was a big one and had been divided into flats all of which were rented out. We had to pay a month's rent in advance as did everyone else. Mrs Nikyforuk, the woman we had met on the first day, and who I thought was our landlady took our first month's rent and said,

"It's not my house. It really belongs to my mother-in-law who lives on the other side of town. I look after it for her – clean it and rent it out. I live in the house across the avenue. If you folks need anything just come to me but as a rule my mother-in-law comes once a month to collect the rent."

I took an instant liking to Jean Nikyforuk. She had a plain unpretentious honesty about her, was friendly and exuded a pleasant laid-back air. Gradually I learned about the difficult life she had. But inspite of her own difficulties she was always helpful to us and was able to supply much of the information we needed. Fortunately for us she had a Scottish grandfather who was still living at ninety and for whom she had a high regard. I had begun to discover it was all right to ask Canadians a lot about their personal life – what wages they earned etc, but you didn't inquire in to their origins unless they offered the information.

182

I am not quite sure why this was a taboo subject but perhaps it had something to do with people trying very hard to be Canadian and forget their ethnic differences. Perhaps, also, because many people who had been here for several generations had an Indian somewhere in their background. Canada wasn't as old as America. They hadn't begun to boast about it yet.

One day when we had been in Edmonton almost a month, a knock came to the door and without giving anyone time to answer, in walked a complete stranger. She was old and wrinkled as a walnut – a straggle of bones with a long pointed nose and a small thin grim mouth. She was dressed completely in black – a long black skirt, a black coat and black kerchief covering iron grey hair – our landlady! She spoke in broken English and said she had come for the rent.

Ronald had left me money to pay and I went into the bedroom to get it. When I came back she was making her way round the kitchen-cum-living-room peering into everything.

"Ze sink has grease," she said screwing up her nose. She opened the oven door where an apple pie had bubbled up and dripped onto the enamel tray the night before.

"Ze oven ees dirty," she said. Quite unabashed she kept on tramping through the house and reached the children's bedroom. The beds were as yet unmade – the floor a muddle of toys and clothes.

"Untidy," she said. "Ess a mess. Better you must do eef you weesh to leeve in my property."

I was too stunned at this intrusion of privacy to say anything. She took her rent and left as quickly as she could banging the door behind her.

After she left my indignation rose. "Damned cheek," I thought. "Old witch and considering too the price we pay for this basement flat. It's not exactly cheap."

I was still simmering when Ronald came home at tea time. He could see I was upset.

"Old bat!" he said. "Much more of that and we'll move elsewhere."

I calmed down – didn't say much more, not wanting to get Ronald upset. I didn't want to move again so soon.

"Maybe I'll have a word with Jean – see what she says. Perhaps I could give the rent to her."

When I mentioned it, Jean was fairly non-committal.

"I guess she loses a lot of tenants that way – makes my job more difficult. But no, she'll be round to collect the rent – insists on doing it."

I said no more about it but resolved that everything would be spick and span the next time she came.

A lot happened in those first two months in Edmonton. Richard was six now – old enough to go to school. A couple of days before he started, snow had fallen in earnest making everything into a Christmas card. The sidewalk was passable with galoshes, the roads became something between packed snow and hard beaten ice.

"However am I going to take him to school?" I asked Jean. "Ronald needs the car. He has to be at the office at eight and I can't push a pram along these sidewalks."

"We sure don't use prams here at this time of year – sledges are much easier. I'll lend you one of mine."

And so I set off with Richard, Michael, Ronnie and Mahri-Louise one September morning to take Richard to his first day at school. The sun shone as it mostly always did in this part of the world. The sky was incurably blue. Everything – gardens, houses, streets – were clothed in snow which sparkled in the sunlight. The houses along both sides of the wide avenue stood out in the clearest of air. There was no smoke or dampness to form any sort of haze.

I left Richard at the new modern school where a teacher took over. There were tears in my eyes at this first big separation from my first born. I didn't want him to notice – didn't want to upset him and I don't think he did notice, so eager was he to take on the new experience.

"Come back at three o'clock," I was told. I was there on the dot – apprehensively expecting Richard to be somewhat subdued and frantic to see me. A surprise awaited me. He was very nonchalant about it all – said he had had a good day. Refused to walk home with me and his motley crew of brothers and a baby sister lying in a sledge. He was a big boy now – walked several paces ahead – pretending he wasn't with us.

Now that my mother had our new address she had written saying how glad she was that we had got somewhere to live in Edmonton and that Ronald had got a job. I hadn't mentioned that it was on commission basis only. That would only have worried her.

"Perhaps it will be easier for you to get Mahri-Louise christened now. If you are looking for a Godmother, Thelma, the daughter of our next door neighbours, the Greys, is living in Edmonton just now. Her husband has a job with the Hudson Bay Company," mother wrote.

I didn't know Thelma well. Her people hadn't always been neighbours of mother's and, by the time they came to live next door, I was nursing and only saw Thelma occasionally. However, glad to have some contact with home I got in touch. Thelma would be delighted to be Godmother. I had just joined the Presbyterian church in Edmonton. It was at Jean Nikyforuk's suggestion. Because of her Presbyterian grandfather she was an active member.

"We sure don't use prams here at this time of year – sledges are much easier."

"We've sure got a nice young minister just now," she said.

Like the school the Church was only a block away. New but built in a traditional style with which I was familiar. The services weren't as familiar. They were higher Church than back home, more like the Episcopal services. The minister was helpful about the christening.

I told him about Thelma.

"You don't need to have a Godmother nowadays. The whole congregation takes the promises but it's fine by me if you want one – just fine.

The day of the christening arrived filled with sunshine. I dressed Mahri-Louise in the long white voile gown that the others had been christened in and wrapped her in a spider fine shawl that my sister-in-law had knitted for me. Mahri-Louise was a pretty pink and white baby with blond hair and big blue eyes. She looked prettier than ever in her long christening gown. The service went well. Mahri wasn't one to cry at the wrong times. A contented child she didn't cry much at all. After the christening the minister held her high and walked round the church showing her off. Everyone stood up and promised they would help to look after her. The emotion of the moment gave me a warm glow inside even although I knew in my heart of hearts that this wasn't how life was. People under certain circumstances make promises that they can't keep. But no thought of that then. It was a happy day and we went back to our basement flat for a simple tea of cookies and cake.

Chapter 27

A Clinic, a Countryman and a Cross Landlady

In those days no way could we have called Edmonton a beautiful city. It may have been the location that was wrong – a city grown from a lonely Hudson Bay fort set in a huge rolling landscape. The Rockies were nowhere to be seen. To the north there was no other town of comparable size between it and the north pole. The Saskatchewan River ran through Edmonton, a pale uninteresting river that left no impression on the mind other than a snakelike greyness. Over it spanned the High Level Bridge, a clever piece of engineering, carrying both road and rail traffic and connecting the dissected city. This area got very congested at busy times.

Jasper Avenue, the main street, was a fine one broad and long with substantial shops on either side. The government buildings down town were also impressive but of no great age. Occasionally Ronald would look after the children while I went into the city centre to do some shopping but I soon discovered this was an expensive and time-consuming exercise. Several blocks from where we lived there was a new hypermarket – something that was unheard of in the part of Scotland I came from in these days. We learned to shop within its vast new precincts as everyone else did in the area.

Edmonton had been well planned using the grid system and what appeared to be unlimited space. For the most part schools were new and well built and Edmonton boasted a university of which all citizens were justly proud. Edmontonians were keen on the idea of culture.

The feeling of space it gave you was what I liked most about the city. Out in the suburbs especially no house was too near another. There were few fences. In winter, back gardens became ice-rinks for children to skate and practise ice hockey on. Jean Nykiforuk's back garden just across the road from us, had one such ice-rink. Her children, most of whom were older than ours, took the boys in hand. Jean had two sons and six daughters ranging in age from from six to seventeen. I never saw the oldest one. She was working and living in Toronto but the next two were teenage girls – dark haired beauties with long legs and graceful carriages. The younger girls by contrast were rounder faced. I once said to Jean,

"You'd almost think you had two separate families."

"I have. The mother of the oldest three was French. She died young." I got no further information at the time but learned later that Jean had married their father when they were all very young and had five more children. She never complained but it was apparent that both her mother-in-law and her husband gave her a hard time. The French Goddess was dead. Jean was obviously considered less than perfect. It was Jean who got my admiration.

By the end of two months in Edmonton things were going reasonably well. Ronald had been able to sell one or two properties and we had enough money to pay rent and living expenses. However I was feeling tired after the strain of the past few months. I gradually stopped breast feeding Mahri-Louise earlier than the others. With the advice of Jean I put her on Carnation milk.

"That's really all we have here," she said. "The mothers all use it."

I tried it but suspected that Carnation milk did not altogether agree with Mahri-Louise. I suggested putting her on cow's milk.

"No – you sure can't do that – not yet awhile – too young – seven months at least," Jean told me and so I persevered with the Carnation milk.

About this time Richard brought a virus back from school rather different from the ones we were accustomed to back in Scotland. It ran its course and was gone. Apart from myself, only Mahri-Louise was left with after-effects – not serious but she had a cold that refused to clear up. Also she had a nasty rash on her bottom which remained even after being left with nappies off for long periods.

"If I was you," Jean advised. "I would take her to the clinic. It's only two blocks away and you don't have to pay."

The clinic, like so much we had found in Edmonton was new, spacious and clean. It smelled strongly of antiseptic. I waited my turn in the queue of anxious mothers and snivelling children. My turn at last. A sharp faced nurse who barely looked at me, told me briskly to take the child's clothes off. I did so. She took one look at Mahri's red bottom.

"Her bottom's very red," she said. "What *have* you been doing to her – tut tut, you young mothers!"

I wasn't feeling well that morning. I had not completely got over the effects of the virus myself. A telling-off was too much – the last thing I needed. I burst into tears. All of a sudden the tone of the questioning changed.

"You folk new around here?"

"Yes," I said.

"Where do you live?"

I told her

"A basement flat?"

"Yes."

"Well that's what's keeping the cold going – not healthy. Bad air. Where do you come from?"

"Scotland."

"When did you come over?"

"Last February."

"Who are your sponsors?"

A wave of fear went through me. I felt the cold questioning of the KGB. I told her who our sponsors were but said nothing of having left their protection. Would she get us into trouble? Now that Ronald had found a job that he liked I wanted nothing to upset things. I wished I had never come.

She handed me a jar of cream to help clear up Mahri's rash and told me to keep her warm and on high pillows when she was sleeping.

"I'll be along in a week or two," she said, "to see how she is and how you are making out."

"No need," I said. "I'll bring her back if she gets no better."

"I'll be along," she said. "We have to watch you immigrants."

Her voice was cold and harsh. I shuddered.

I didn't say much to Ronald that evening not wanting to give him any more worries than he already had, but I made a new resolution. When the health visitor came to see me she would find nothing wrong. I was quite convinced myself that it was the Carnation milk that was disagreeing with Mahri-Louise. I put her on cow's milk. The rash on her bottom disappeared. Although she had been on solids for some time she still wasn't eating much. I asked Jean's advice.

"I'd a kid like that once. Try her on squash. They all like squash."

I hadn't heard of it before but I bought a tin of squash baby food from the local drugstore. I opened it and was immediately captivated by its glorious orange colour. I tasted it – no taste at all, neither sweet, sour or salty. I had little hope of Mahri-Louise liking it. I was wrong. She lapped it up – couldn't get enough. Soon she began to improve on a diet of cow's milk and squash but she still had the persistent sniffles. I thought the nurse was probably right. The rather fuggy air of our basement flat was not the best environment for her. Fresh air would do her more good than anything else. I had learned by this time from various Canadian women, that taking babies outside before the age of one was anathema to most Albertans because of below zero temperatures or too bright sunlight. It had become almost a superstition. At home my babies had always spent a lot of their lives outside in the pram. Certainly it had never got as cold as here. I wrapped Mahri-louise up carefully, insulated her pram with newspaper and put it in the porch which was sheltered from the little wind that there was. I went out often to see that she wasn't cold. Her sniffles cleared up quickly.

When the nurse eventually came everything was in order. The house was as sparkling as I could make it. I had to do it for the witch's next visit anyway. I was hanging nappies up on the rope beside the boiler when the health nurse came. I had paid particular attention to getting them really white of late. When she walked in unexpectedly they were as white as the snow in the front gardens. She examined Mahri-Louise whose skin had begun to glow with being out in the fresh air.

"She looks a lot better," she said almost accusingly.

"Yes," I said adding nothing.

"You seem to be coping well enough."

"Oh I'm fine," I said.

"I won't be back," she said. "But if you need me you know where I am."

Under my breath I answered, And I won't be back, and breathed a thankful sigh of relief.

About ten weeks after getting our basement flat, Adrian from Sandy Hills breezed in. We had sent him our address but this was the first time we had seen or heard from him.

"I've quit," he said. "Fed up with Jacobs' nonsense and I'm fed up with farming. Don't want to be a dirt farmer or a slave all my life. That's not what I came out to Canada for. I'm getting married soon and I want to get a job in the city. Gloria wants to come to the city also. She is tired of the 'sticks'. Can I stay with you for a bit until I get a job and a place of my own?"

"Certainly," Ronald said. He was pleased to see the bright Adrian again. "I'd better ask the landlady but I don't see how she'd mind. There's an extra room."

I liked the idea also. Apart from good company it would give us a bit of extra cash. I asked Jean if she thought it would be all right.

The next time the witch came Ronald happened to be in. She had heard about our lodger from Jean and kicked up a great song and dance.

"Look at all zee extra electricity he use for plugging in zee car and other tings," she said. I'm not made of zee money. If he stay you'll have to pay to me some more." And she mentioned an exorbitant sum.

Ronald had been intending to say nothing to her about her unwelcome intrusions until we had become a bit more established but this was the last straw.

"All right, we'll pay for the time he has been here but you better start looking for another tenant. This is the last month's rent you'll get from me. We're leaving!" Ronald's confidence was growing.

Chapter 28

Up North

Rounding a bend in the road, after travelling along its straight, dusty gravel tracks for what seemed like for ever, the lake suddenly appeared as blue as the June sky and catching sun-diamonds in its watery net. The great expanse of water immediately in front of us was surrounded by trees, poplar and birch, each fragile leaf of each tree a mirror from which the sun reflected. My heart missed a beat. This could be Scotland on a sunny day. Ronald's words echoed my thoughts.

"Like some loch back home, isn't it?"

It was mid afternoon on a Friday in June. We wanted to be at the lake in time for potential customers at the weekend. In front of the lake, at the top of a steep gradient, not quite big enough to be called a hill, stood a house – a baronial type mansion fashioned from wood. We had been told there was a house by the lake but were surprised at its size and appearance. It had been built by an Englishman, all his own effort, earlier in the century. The story went that he had lived here on his own, a recluse for thirty years or more before drowning himself in the lake – no reason given but maybe loneliness had at last got to him. It was miles from anywhere – no road in or out. It wasn't until recently, since Empire Real Estate had bought it in fact, that a road was being put in and it wasn't finished yet. What puzzled me, even more than its remoteness, was why build so baronial a mansion just for one. Was it a dream he had? Did the lake remind him of home? Had he been a remittance man, someone from a well-to-do, respectable family paid to stay away in another land because of some misdemeanour in his youth – unable ever to go home?

With the passage of time the house had taken on a

ramshackle appearance. Wide wooden steps in need of repair, led up to a large wooden door standing open when we arrived. Only the screen door remained closed. Sitting at the door on a listing veranda, in the warm afternoon sunshine, was a middle-aged man. He was dressed in a pair of tight-fitting jeans, the belt of which had slipped below his over-large belly. His top half was bare. His chest was broad and muscular as were his shoulders. He had the permanent tan of someone who worked perpetually out of doors. His round weather-beaten face had a stubble of beard. The sinews on his strong neck stuck out like tight ropes.

We let the boys out of the car to get rid of some of their pent-up energy. Ronald ran up the wooden steps, two at a time, to introduce himself. I followed more sedately

"I'm Ron Gillies from Empire Real Estate," he said.

The man didn't move from the wooden box he was sitting on. Beside him stood a crate of beer. Before acknowledging Ronald's greeting he popped an empty beer bottle in the crate and took out a full one easing the top off with his teeth. He put the bottle to his mouth, took a swig, the liquid went down easily.

"I'm Glug-Glug Stevannuk," he said, obviously revelling in the Christian name he had adopted. "Here, have a beer." He took another bottle from the crate, opened it in the same way and handed it to Ronald. Stevannuk was the man who had bought the lake a couple of years back and then sold it to Empire Real Estate. He had a house in Edmonton but in the summer he and his wife came out here to live.

"Tanya," he called through the screen door, "the Real Estate folk." She came out rather reluctantly, I thought, to speak to us – a gaunt thin women with eyes that had known hardship.

"You folks going back tonight?" she asked after the initial introductions.

"We're staying for the weekend. We've got a tent with us. Where would be best to pitch it?"

"Anywhere you like!" Stevannuk answered spreading out his arms. Better in the woods at the back than down at the water front. It's warmer. Mighty cold wind comes up from that lake sometimes."

"Any bears around?" Ronald asked.

"Haven't seen any for the longest time," he replied. But that aint't to say one mightn't come snuffling around. You gotta gun?"

"Nope," said Ronald.

By this time Tanya had already disappeared back into the house. "Wait here I'll git you one. You can have it for the summer."

Stevannuk got up off the wooden box, straightened himself painfully and followed Tanya. It wasn't long till he came back out again carrying an old blunderbuss and handed it to Ronald.

"Already primed and ready to blast. Shouldn't need it but you sure never can tell," he said.

We found a clearing in the primaeval forest that lay behind the lake. It was a good place to pitch our tent being not far from the big house but out of sight of it. All around us were scrub birches, poplars and fir trees. Before Ronald did anything else he unloaded the blunderbuss. He had always had a healthy respect for guns.

"I'll keep the ammunition by me. I'll soon load it if I need to."

The boys were excited and helped their Dad erect the tent, vigorously knocking in the tent pegs. We were quite comfortable that first night as we were sheltered from the wind that sprung up from the loch. We had brought plenty of blankets for, although it was officially summer and hot during the day, it could still be cold at night. Sometimes, later on in the season, it felt as if the night wind came straight from the Arctic as it probably did. Eventually all the children fell asleep – Mahri in her pram within the tent as it kept her off the cold ground.

Once they were all asleep Ronald and I crawled out into the night. Only a thin sliver of moon shone in the black watersilk sky. We stood on the edge of the trees and looked out towards the lake dimly discernible in the darkness. I rubbed my eyes. Were they playing tricks? Tiny flickerings of light appeared, disappeared.

"Ron, am I seeing things? Tiny flecks of red light?"

"I see them too – must be fireflies – didn't know we would get them here."

Next morning I rose to an even more delightful surprise. Not far from the tent a clump of wild flowers were in bloom. I went closer to admire them and stood spellbound. Beside one of the blossoms, suspended in air – a humming bird was sipping nectar. I couldn't imagine anything more exquisite or more aerodynamically marvellous. At times this minute bird seemed to be capable of standing still in the air, at others flying backwards with apparent ease. I hadn't expected to see humming birds so far north.

That first Saturday we wondered if anyone would be interested in lake side lots so far off the beaten track. We waited apprehensively. Empire Real Estate had done its advertising well. A surprising number of families in Pontiacs and Chevrolets with pitted windows and dented doors drove in – the women replete with picnic baskets – the men with axes for chopping firewood. It was obvious they were going to stay for the day. One or two families were genuinely interested in the lots that had been marked out at the edge of the Lake – some of the trees had been cleared from these lots but not all as everyone wanted a rustic appearance. By evening, as the roar of cars rumbled into the distance, things looked hopeful for a sale or two. Ronald looked relieved and happy.

"Lets go fishing boys," he said, "catch something for the tea."

He had brought his fishing rod and made three simple ones up for the boys from poplar wands he had cut from the forest, string and hooks brought from home, foreseeing such an eventuality. Much to my surprise they all came back with fish. Wee Ronnie was jumping up and down with excitement.

"Me caught fish – me caught fish," he repeated excitedly. It was quite a big one too. Ronald remarked on how easy they were to catch.

"They're hungry," he said. "Either that or they are completely unaware of the dangers of men."

I had brought one or two pans to cook in over a brushwood fire but no frying pan.

"How will I cook them?" I said. Ronald came up with a bright idea.

"All these newspapers I've brought to read – I'll use some of the pages for cooking the fish in. I learned how to do it while camping in my boy scout days."

He took the newspaper down to the edge of the lake and came back with it soaking wet. He wrapped the fish in the wet newspaper – made five neat parcels. The boys in the meantime had been gathering sticks for a fire. There was no shortage of burnable wood around. Soon the fire was blazing. The air smelt of Gypsies. When the flames died down a bit Ronald eased the fish packets into the red embers.

"When the paper dries they're ready," he said. In what seemed a remarkably short time we dragged them out of the fire with long sticks and left them to cool until they were fit to handle. They were the sweetest fish I had ever tasted.

A few families found their way to the lake on Sunday also but this time, rather to our surprise, instead of staying there until evening they all left in the early afternoon. When the roar of departing cars and trucks died down all was primaeval silence again.

"They're in a hurry today," Ronald remarked." Must be because of work tomorrow."

We had planned to stay another night – return to Edmonton in the morning. Again we gathered sticks and lit a fire on which to cook our evening meal. Wood smoke went curling up above the trees until suddenly the brushwood leapt into flame. When the fire died down somewhat, I made two small nests of burning embers. On one I placed the kettle on the other a pan of wieners and beans. It wasn't until we were having our evening meal that we heard the rumble of thunder and were aware of black clouds.

"Looks as if we might get rain," said Ronald. "I'm told June is the one month you can be sure of getting it."

Remember the thunder storm at Sandyhills?" I said, "That was June wasn't it?"

Ronald chose to ignore that memory. "We'll be all right. Hopefully the main storm will pass us by."

Huge raindrops began to fall.

"I'll bet this was why folks scarpered off so quickly," I said. "They knew this was coming"

"Don't be so pessimistic," said Ronald.

We hurried the children into the tent and got them ready for bed. The thunder sounded nearer and the rain was getting heavier. Blue zig zag streaks shot earthward. We saw them through the white walls of the tent. "If you don't touch the tent the rain won't come through," Ronald told the boys.

Mahri-Louise, unperturbed by the thunder, was fast asleep in her pram. Richard and Ronnie thought it was exciting and wanted to watch. Michael wasn't so sure. He lay down covering his head with a blanket. The rain was really lashing down now and it was dark – very dark. I kept the torch on to give us some light. All of a sudden the tent flap opened and I saw in the torchlight a face – the severe face of Tanya Stevannuk, wet grey hair sticking to the sides of her gaunt and wrinkled cheeks.

"Sure is some storm," she said. "You folks better come on inside for the night. Bring your bedding with you but wait till we get a lull in the rain." With that she vanished as quickly as she had come.

We collected everything together, waited until the rain eased a little and made a dash for it. Everyone was carrying something. Ronald was pushing the pram over the rough ground but still Mahri Louise didn't waken. Tanya had changed into dry clothes and was waiting for us. She showed us into a large room panelled in wood. The room had no furniture or carpet. The boys lay down on the floor and I covered them with the now damp blankets. With all the movement Mahri had wakened. We lay down taking her beside us. I won't say it was the most comfortable night we ever spent. The boards had an ungiving hardness. The undulating earth floor in the tent had been more comfortable. Mahri was restless for quite some time and I, with a new baby on the way, had a feeling of nausea but we were grateful to be out of the storm. We had been told that Ukranians were hard people to deal with in business but when people were in real difficulties could be helpful in a practical way This we were finding out for ourselves.

Next morning the sun was shining as if it had never shone before. Every blade of grass, every leaf had its own personal clear pearl of water clinging to it – a tiny crystal ball for the sun to dance on. Tanya had given us breakfast before we returned to the tent – coffee and home baked bread and saskatoon jam. Back at the tent we found everything soaking. We all walked about in bare feet – shoes would have been soaked through in a very short time.

We had to get packed up as soon as possible as Ronald had a customer to meet in the early afternoon back in Edmonton. I packed things into the car. On the way out from the lake we passed Stevannuk. Ronald rolled down the window.

"Thanks for everything," we said." We'll be back next week."

"You folks'll sure be lucky if you get out that road today," he said.

"We'll try," said Ronald "must get back. I've an appointment to keep later today."

The road had looked smooth and dusty when we arrived and we knew there were several miles of it before we got on to the proper gravel road. Stevannuk was right. To begin with we slithered and slid along in the mud. If it had remained level land all the way we might have managed to get out but it went down a steep slope shortly after we left. Ronald stopped the car.

"You're never going to make it," I said pessimistically. "We might manage to slither to the bottom in that sea of mud but we're never going to get up the other side."

For once Ronald, an expert driver, listened.

"I guess you're right," he said.

We turned and while doing so almost landed in the ditch. We slithered and slipped our way back. Glug Glug was still there with a knowing grin on his face.

"Didn't I tell you guys?" he said. "You'll have to wait till it dries up. No way can you get out unless you hoof it."

I had brought enough food to last for a few days as we had been warned this might happen. We just didn't want to believe it. Ronald erected the tent again then took the boys fishing while Mahri and I lay in the bright sunlight and fell asleep to the noisy quarrelling of grackles.

Next morning we woke to a heavy dew. Barefeet again was the order of the morning. Again the sun leapt off a million tiny crystals Soon after I dressed, Tanya appeared carrying a huge plateful of hot scones.

"Thought you might be a little short of food seein' as how you didn't figure about the storm," she said. "You'll get out today, I guess – road's dried up a lot. Tanya knew what she was talking about.

Long afterwards I wrote a poem remembering that first summer at the lake . . .

> Mention fireflies,
> I think of Nakamun;
> that Indian lake
> Beyond the reservation.
> Mention Nakamun,
> I think of fireflies -
> sudden sparks in the dark,
> phosphorescent light,
> undreamed of experience
> thrilling the blood,
> conjuring possibilities,
> questions in the night.
> Mention fireflies and Nakamun
> I think of schools of strange fish
> in hazed light beneath blue,
> a hummingbirds backward flight,
> the loons eerie laughter
> over sunset's red water,
> a white tent full of children
> asleep in the forest. . .
> say firefly
> say Nakamun
> say firefly
> say Nakamun
> say firefly. . .
> A spark in the dark
> of infinite possibility.

Once, at an even later date, after reading this poem out at a meeting, a lady rushed up to me at the end and said -

"I was in Alberta in the nineteen fifties and your poem brings it all back to me but for one thing. What about the bears?"

Well, I guess I had too many other distractions to worry about bears and all the time we were at Nakamun we didn't actually see one.

Chapter 29

Carmen

Most weekends that summer found us at the lake. Sometimes it was difficult to get there due to lack of money to buy petrol, even although petrol was cheap in Canada. One Friday we had absolutely no money but by this time we had a few friends. Ronald found the Canadian men difficult to get to know. He didn't have much in common with them and felt more akin to the Germans. It seemed as though they spoke the same language although they didn't always in terms of speech.

Ted Shroers was one such friend. He hadn't been in Alberta much longer than we had but he could speak understandable English. He had a wife and family and worked for the Hudson Bay Company. His pay wasn't good but it was regular and they were thrifty and managed. Ronald knew he could ask him for a loan.

On that particular Friday when we were completely broke we called at Ted's house on the way to Nakamun.

"Five dollars," Ronald asked for. "Five dollars would do. It's just for gas and a bit over in case we get stuck somewhere."

The houses in the street we now lived in, running along the top of the avenue we had just left, weren't so picturesque. They were an odd mixture – some new, some old by Canadian standards, some low, some high and mostly made of wood. The people were from various backgrounds. A few were Canadian but mostly they were of different nationalities. Some were recent immigrants like ourselves. It was a moving population with people always coming and going. We had several things in common – mostly we were young, lacked money, had young children and had unfortunately, beyond the gardens, a busy road to contend with.

Carmen

A mother I got to know well lived next door in a flat in a big wooden house. The house was owned by a Ukranian couple whose children had grown and gone. They had divided it up into flats – lived in one themselves and let the other two out. Carmen and her three children had come to live in the basement flat several months after we had moved into our house. Her two boys Tommy aged seven and Billy aged five soon struck up an aquaintance with our boys. Carmen was younger than me. She was twenty three. Tommy was born when she was sixteen. She was pretty with dark Spanish hair and soft Spanish eyes and had a neat figure that gave the lie to having had three children. All summer she wore smart blouses and figure-hugging shorts that couldn't have got much shorter. Men turned twice to look at her. Her boys were often in our garden so inevitably I got to know her. Occasionally she too would pop over for a coffee bringing her little girl Chillas with her. One day not long after our first visit to the lake I confided to her that I was pregnant again. This unexpectedly released the predicament she was in. She told me her troubles.

"I got married to Elmer at sixteen – had to – was expecting Tommy and then I had another two – but he was a right bum – bullied me – beat me up from time to time. Suppose it was a bit my fault as well. I must have been unbearable to live with at times. Eventually it got all too much and I took myself off to the high level bridge. Some guy who happened to be around stopped me from jumping off and then I was in the mental hospital for six months getting over a nervous breakdown. Mother looked after the kids. Elmer had blown off with someone else – didn't want him around anyway. For a while they couldn't get me out of my depression – had the most god-awful job. They tried everything but I just didn't care whether I lived or died – I wished I could die – didn't even care about the kids and Chillas was just a baby. Eventually they tried a treatment using insulin – don't know how it worked but it did. I began to care again – bother how I looked and wanted to see my children. Everyday I got better. Mother was a brick, a tower of strength. I don't know how I would have managed without her but it was all a bit much for her I think. She doesn't keep too well so here I am now in a

201

flat of my own with the kids. I love them now more than anything else on earth, but haven't I gone and made a god-darn mess of things again – no one to blame but myself.

"Dirk's a big fellow – terrific shoulders – nice to be with at the start – nice to me to begin with but he's turning out like Elmer only worse. I think there's a screw loose somewhere – God can I pick em! This guy can get real violent at times. Cut my phone wires the other night. You sure must have heard the commotion – me screaming at him. I've told him to go but I sure don't know if I'll get quit of him that easy. Worst of all I'm three months pregnant with his child. I really don't know what to do. He's a funny guy. He sure seems keen to have a kid but I haven't told him. There's only one way I can see out of the mess and that's to get rid of the baby and then Dirk. I'm trapped. There's no other way I can move. If I have his child he'll never leave me alone. I know it. If he ever finds out that I had an abortion he'll either kill me or tell the authorities and they'll take all my children away. It's illegal to have an abortion in Canada and I'll be classed as being not fit to be a mother."

"Oh they couldn't possibly do that," I said shocked at the idea.

"Oh yes they will," she said. "You'd be surprised at the reasons they give for taking your children from you over to foster parents. I can't tell my mother about the baby. She's a strong Catholic – would see it as a great sin and so do I but what else can I do? I can't go to the priest. I know what he'll say, or the doctor. It would just be a downright No. I'm trapped – I think it'll have to be an abortion – you're a nurse. Could tell me how it's done – help me?"

For a moment or two I was stunned into silence.

"I got my State Registered Nurse's Certificate," I said. "Had my name down to do maternity but never did it as I got married instead but, Carmen think again. I worked in the gynaecological ward for a while – saw a number of abortions done for different reasons and saw the heartache it could bring. And worse than that, some came in when things had gone wrong. I'm sure things can't be as bad as you make out – there must be some other way."

Wrapped up in her own dilemma Carmen wasn't really

listening to what I was saying.

"If I managed to do it myself," she continued, "and things didn't go quite right, would you help me? What would you do if I started to bleed for instance? I've heard there's a danger."

There's only one thing I could do," I said sadly. "Get you to the hospital as soon as possible."

I wished I could have been more helpful to her at the time – said something that would have given her a ray of hope but could think of nothing that she would listen to.

I didn't see much of her in the next month. I was worried about her but there was nothing I could do. She had taken the children to stay with her mother for a week or two. I hoped she would feel able to confide in her. It was several weeks before I saw her again, still neat in shorts and a red blouse. She had an ashen pallor about her but she was hanging up the washing with her usual quick movements. I could see there was something the matter but couldn't intrude as Dirk was hanging about in the background. I wasn't sure if she was speaking to me or not after my refusal to help. Next morning, however, when I thought Dirk would be off to work, I felt compelled to go and see her. I knocked at her door. Tommy answered.

"Your mum in?" I asked. Carmen's ashen face appeared at the door.

"Thought it was Dirk and was just about to give him a blasting. I gave him the final boot last night. Told him he hadn't to come back on any account but I should be so lucky – expecting him back at any moment. I've told him I'll get the police if he cuts my phone wires again."

"You all right?" I asked. "I saw you hanging out the washing yesterday and thought you looked pale."

"Come in," she said. "Tommy, you and Billy go out and play."

"I've done it," she said. "Did it myself. Got someone I know in Edmonton to tell me how – used Sunlight soap."

"Are you all right?"

"Well I guess I'm on the mend. It was real scary for a while – lost a lot of blood and had to keep going so that no one would suspect anything – especially Dirk – just said I had some germ but I've done it and no one knows but you. I feel terrible about

203

killing the baby." Tears slid down her cheeks. "Would have had it if I could have seen any way out. How I envy you your one. Mine might have been born in the same week."

I was a loss for adequate words. I got up and put an arm round her shoulders giving them a squeeze.

"I'm sorry I could do so little to help. All I can say now is eat as well as you can and take iron tablets for a while to build your body up again. Is there anything practical that I can do now? I asked.

Carmen was silent for a moment.

"Well there is something. Don't quite like asking you. . ."

"What is it?" I asked.

"My divorce to Elmer has just come through," Carmen continued. "And he's off to the Dew Line. He's got someone else with a kid on the way, poor women. I'm supposed to get maintenance for myself and the kids but knowing Elmer . . . Can't rely on it and I can't ask my folks for any more. I'll have to get a job. A friend thinks he'll be able to get me one in an oil company – typist cum secretary – quite good pay and I could do it. The problem is the kids. Mother can't take them. I was wondering if you could take them on – I'd pay you of course – as near the going rate as I'm able. Shouldn't think I'll be starting for another month and by that time Tommy and Billy will both be at school. It would be eight in the morning till five in the evening – what do you think?"

Normally I would have hesitated – asked for time before I answered – discussed it with Ron, but these were no ordinary times for either Carmen or myself. I very much wanted to help her but also, inadvertently, I had stumbled on something that could help us – give us some steady money. I knew that rates for baby sitting were good in Canada. Tommy and Billy got on well with our boys. Tommy, a big stout, cheery fellow with a stomach that went before him and an army haircut, looked several years older than his seven years. He always wanted to be the boss telling the others what they should be playing at but usually managed to make what he wanted to do sound so exciting that they wanted to do it anyway. Billy, also a well-built fellow with an army haircut but smaller, was by nature sulkier and more truculent. You always knew what Tommy was thinking but were less sure about Billy. Was he harbouring resentments? Of the two, although he was much more disobedient, I always preferred Tommy. Chillas, now quietly sitting on her mother's knee sucking a bottle, was a thin slip of a girl – pale with lank hair, a permanently running nose and, according to her mum, suffering from earache.

"I'll have a go," I said. "But if I do find it too much for me with the baby coming and all – you'll understand. I'll give you plenty warning so that you can find someone else."

"Gee that sure is wonderful," said Carmen slipping Chillas off her knee and putting her bottle on the table to give me a big hug. "It'll just be so goddam handy having you so close."

Chapter 30

Surprise Day

"We'll need to find another lodger," I said to Ronald one day shortly after Adrian's wedding.

"I'll put an ad in the paper today," said Ronald.

I was apprehensive about the outcome. Who would we get – some immigrant who could barely speak English – some roughneck – some brash Canadian? Would they be pleased with our kind of household – all these kids – a rickety house on its last legs? A house where children could poke knitting needles through the walls and reach fresh air and did once or twice when they discovered the knitting needles I had brought from home.

"I suppose we could put 'Would suit a British immigrant'," I suggested to Ronald.

"No we couldn't," said Ronald. "That limits the thing far too much. Besides very few British immigrants come to Alberta – sensible people," Ronald threw in as an afterthought.

It was with trepidation that I waited for the phone to ring. A phone was a necessity for us because of Ronald's business. Sometimes I got calls during the day for Ronald. In the afternoon of the day the advertisement went into the paper the phone rang. Apprehensively I lifted the receiver.

"You have a room for rent?" To my astonishment the voice had an unmistakable Scottish burr.

"Yes," I said. "We had a lodger but he left last week to get married and we are looking for someone to replace him."

"You're Scottish?" the voice at the other end sounded as surprised as myself.

"Yes," I said.

"I'll be round," he said, "this evening to see the place if that's OK?"

"Certainly," I said. "My husband will be in. Perhaps I should warn you that we have quite a few kids – if you don't mind kids?"

"I don't," he said.

Henry came that evening at the arranged time. Ronald took an immediate liking to him. Here at last was someone he could relate to. Henry was about our age, of medium height with light brown hair and blue eyes, good features and a pleasant smile. His second name was Brown. It suited him. He saw the sparsely furnished room badly in need of decoration and took it. He liked the price which I had made reasonable and he liked the fact that we were immigrants like himself. He told us a little about himself.

"This is my second time out in Canada – came out for the adventure and to see if I could make a bit of money but it's not easy getting a job. I didn't get the job I came out for but managed to get another one. Fell out with the boss not long ago. He was a right ogre." Here Ronald could sympathise.

"Sheer chance that I met this fellow whom I'd worked with last time I was in Canada. I was crossing the road, wondering what I was going to do next, when his car came round the corner and screeched to a halt. He asked what I was working at now. I told him the story. He said I should try the construction firm where he was working. They were hiring on one or two just now and the job would last through the winter months. I went along and got the job. It's on this side of town so I needed to change my accommodation."

Henry said he would get his things together – move in next day.

When he had gone I saw the lines relax on Ronald's high forehead.

"That was a lucky shot," he said, "and I like him. He is one of these rare people who is totally genuine – someone you can trust."

"He seems tolerant about the kids too," I said. "Even although they were making a racket when he came. He say's he was one of five himself. I think he liked the friendliness of the kids and how Mahri wanted to sit on his knee."

And so Henry came into our lives. Henry was quite different

from Adrian. He travelled light and I had much less washing and ironing to do for him. He never complained about the food and was tolerant with the children. Not that he saw much of them in the week days. Either he stayed in his room and read, fell asleep after a hard day's work, or went down town.

Carmen started work a week before the school took up. A tough week for me but I coped as best I could. Tommy was trying to rule the roost. Billy kept up a sulky silence and Chillas girned all day long. Richard fortunately was looking forward to going to school again. He was growing really tall and self-assured. Michael was four and a half. In Canada children didn't go to school until they were six but Jean Nykiforuk said to me one day,

"They take kids in at five and a half now if they have been at playschool. They watch how they make out and if they do well they take them in."

Because of what she said Ronald and I thought it was important that Michael should go to playschool. Michael was not of the same opinion. He didn't want to go to any kind of school and let it be known by a loud wailing. It upsets me yet when I think about his first days at playschool – his drooping eyelids that made his eyes look sad anyway – his tear-stained face. The play school wasn't far away. To begin with I always went with him but as the winter took hold it got too difficult to dress up and take the little ones on the sledge every morning. Gradually Michael began to accept the play school. The teacher was good with him. To begin with he refused to join in with the others. She put him at a small table by himself and every day drew it a fraction closer to the long one where the rest of the children sat painting, drawing or making things. By Christmas his small table was joined on to their long one and the teacher found to her pleasure that Michael, who had refused to join in the singing or reciting, knew all the words and had been learning all the time.

With Tommy and Billy at school and Michael at play school, I got a bit more time to concentrate on Chillas. I was determined to find out what was wrong with her and make her into a healthy little girl. I got a clue to the problem on the first day I got her.

"Chillas sure isn't much trouble," Carmen told me. "She doesn't eat much but likes her bottle of milk about every hour. She needs to have it – otherwise just biscuits or cake or something, that's all she'll take. It's the same at night with the bottle. I've got to get up two or three times to give her the darn thing."

Every morning before she left Carmen gave me a full baby's bottle of milk and more to top it up with during the day.

It was hard going but gradually I began to succeed in weaning her off it until she was only getting milk out of her bottle twice a day. Gradually I got her on to more nourishing solids. It wasn't however, until two or three weeks after coming to me, that I got to the real root of the problem. One day I thought the milk in Chillas's bottle looked funny. I smelt it. It was off. I didn't give her any that day at all, just poured it out and gave her milk out of Mahri's drinking cup. I didn't wash the bottle wanting to find out what would happen. The following day the bottle came back – refilled but with a sour smell again. Carmen hadn't washed the bottle. I couldn't believe it – Carmen who was so neat and clean in every other way didn't wash or sterilise the bottle properly, just filled it with fresh milk every morning. I stopped giving Chillas milk from the bottle altogether but she was still getting it from her mother. I didn't like to say anything to Carmen so each day I accepted the bottle of milk, poured it out and sterilised the bottle. Chillas began to improve by leaps and bounds. Carmen was delighted.

"My mother sure was a bit dubious about you looking after the kids to begin with," Carmen said to me one day. "Even although I told her you were a nurse. Seemed to think that being a poor immigrant you mightn't give them enough to eat but after seeing Chillas lately and after hearing what Tommy had to eat the other day at your place – well!"

"What did he tell her?" I asked.

"Well he said he had asparagus soup, stewed beef and potatoes, marshmallows, a chocolate biscuit and a slice of water melon."

"They don't always get such a variety," I said. "That was Surprise Day."

209

One evening a week, just before closing time, the super-market sold off cheaply what ever was at the end of its sell-by date. I was always there to pick up the bargains. The following day had been christened 'Surprise Day' by the children because they never knew what they would get.

Chapter 31

Sell the Sizzle, Not the Steak!

Fortunately Ronald was getting some sales. He had sold quite a few lakeside lots during the summer – a farm and one or two acreages. We had enough money to buy another second hand car. The men in the Real Estate office used to laugh at Ronald's old car with its badly pitted windscreen and faded paintwork. The boss, Bill Martin, didn't think it gave the right image for Empire Real Estate. The new used car had a better appearance. We had got a Chevrolet again because despite the age of our first one, it had given a good performance. Ronald was happy because the new one would be less likely to break down in outlandish places. We had taken some awful risks in the old one, sometimes going off to the lake with bald tyres and no spare that was any better, but the old Chevy had seldom let us down.

Ronald was enjoying his job. Empire Real Estate was pleased with his work. He wasn't a high-powered salesman – refused to pressure anyone – the customers trusted him – it worked. He had been taught a lot about the tricks of selling but some of the advice he got he didn't agree with or adhere to. One such piece of advice was what they called 'selling the sizzle not the steak'. Ronald believed honesty was the best policy and stuck to it.

I would have loved to have gone with him from time to time, driving into the countryside. Sometimes he travelled many miles. He came back with tales of the places he had been to – people he had met. He told me about three old brothers living in a shack at Cooking Lake. They were all over seventy and had always lived in comparative isolation. Even yet there was no one very near to them but they were wanting to move further north. To their way of thinking the place was getting congested!

There was another old couple whose shack had burned down

and who now lived in a henhouse. They didn't complain to Ronald about losing almost all their possessions, just mentioned how wonderful it was that their prize possession, the old family bible, had been saved. They owned a quarter section of land and hoped it would bring in enough money to buy a flat in Edmonton.

Another couple were in much the same position. They were both in their eighties and felt no longer able to farm. They had a half section of land to sell. He was a huge man, bent with hard work. She was tiny. They liked to talk to Ronald as many country people did. Ronald was a good listener. They liked to tell him about their lives. Bob, the husband, told how in the beginning he had managed to raise just enough money to buy a half section. The Province handed out parcels of land for very few dollars in these early days. He had to clear the land of trees before he could start any kind of cultivation. He told Ronald how he had done it with the help of his tiny wife. There were areas of muskeg on the land – waterlogged acres where it was necessary to wade through wet sludge up to the waist. At times, when she was out helping him, he lifted her onto his shoulders while wading through the worst bits in case she disappeared out of sight. His wife had been of the greatest help to him. As far as he was concerned she was beyond rubies.

One evening Ronald came home distressed about a family of recent immigrants They were Dutch and had a lot of young children. They kept pigs. Disease had swept through the animals. They were ruined and would have to sell. Their farm was quite far from the railroad. That would make a sale difficult. Ronald was determined to make every effort to sell it for them and get as good a price as possible.

Ronald also came across people who had made it, who perhaps had a nice house on the outskirts of Edmonton which on selling would give them enough money to buy a smaller one in the more temperate climate of Vancouver – the dream of many Edmontonians.

On the whole money was scarce and land was often sold at bargain prices. Ronald would come home some evenings and say,

"What a bargain these folk got today. I wish I had had the money to buy it."

It was through Ronald's job that we got to know an extended family of Scottish immigrants. The MacFarlanes bought a quarter section of land from Ronald up near Lake Nakamun. The land hadn't been cleared and was rather far from the railway but it was cheap. The MacFarlanes paid for it with the wood they took off the land. Ian MacFarlane had a good job with an oil company so it was more or less bought for a holiday place – somewhere to go at the weekends. Back home in Scotland, Jill, his wife, had lived in a village close to our old farm for several years although I had never met her before. It was lovely to have some sort of contact with home again.

As for ourselves, we still felt vulnerable and isolated. What if either of us should fall ill? Fortunately up till now illness had not been much of a problem. Ronald was anxious, however, that I should get fixed up with a doctor because of the forthcoming baby. Adrian had told us that the doctor we had in Sandyhills had come to practise in Edmonton. We decided we could do no better than to go back to him. We found out where he was – the east side of Edmonton – quite a long way from us. We had been told that as a rule, Edmonton's doctors didn't go out on calls much but, in case they had to, liked to have patients in their own area. However we wanted to have him as our doctor if he would have us.

" We won't need you much." I said on my first visit, "We keep pretty healthy" He agreed to take us on.

Not long after I had been to see him Richard came home from school with a sore throat. He was feverish for a day or two until an alarming red rash appeared. I hadn't seen anything like it before but the words scarlet fever came into my head. Reluctantly I called the doctor. All the children were back from school when he came – the racket in the kitchen was dreadful.

"Good gracious how many children have you got?" he said. I explained the situation. He went upstairs to examine Richard.

"How many of the children go to school?" he asked when we came back downstairs.

"Three," I replied, "and Michael goes to playschool."

"Well," he said, "I'm not quite sure what it is but if I put down suspected scarlet fever on my chit of notifiable diseases, all the children will have to stay off school for six weeks. It's the law in Alberta. We'll see how things go. I'm just going to call it a streptococcal throat meantime. Richard is perhaps past the worst. I'll give you these capsules for him and call back in a day or two. If you're worried at all give me a phone."

Richard took a wee while to recover but much to my surprise no one else took it.

In no time at all it seemed the Christmas holidays were upon us and for several days before Christmas I had all the children to entertain. One day at the beginning of the holidays, while suffering the aftermaths of a cold and feeling tired and a bit sorry for myself, I wondered how I was going to cope.

"I must give the children something to do – get them games to play with or something," I said to Ronald one morning. "Would you look after them for ten minutes or so, before you take off, while I go along to the drug store at the corner? It sells all sorts of things."

"I'll go for you if you like," he said

"Thanks but I'd just like to get out of the house for ten minutes," I said and donned my hooded parka.

Heavy with child now I trudged wearily along the snow-covered sidewalk. The man in the drug store was helpful and pleasant. I told him of my plight – had he colouring books, games etc that would keep seven young children amused for a while? He smiled at me and said,

"Now aren't you the lucky one. I had a customer in the other day and she had no children. Folks tell me their troubles you know. She sure would have loved a child but none had come along. You look after seven you say?" He gave a quick glance at my unmistakable bulge, "and there will be more. How interesting life must be for you. How many professions you have to follow – nurse, philosopher, cook, teacher, adviser, – there's sure no end to it – you need to be a bit of everything."

Amazingly I began to feel better. He looked me out some games and colouring books. I walked home with a jaunty step.

How bright the sun was now, how azure the sky, how colourful the houses against the sparkling snow and the few people I met were smiling.

Christmas came and went. We still couldn't afford to give the children much but then neither could Carmen next door so Tommy and Billy weren't lording it over our lot. Then, of course, once more the marvellous parcels came from home. Mother and others had put a great deal of love and thought into what they sent.

Ronald had New Year all arranged early. This time with folk of our own nationality. The MacFarlanes, to whom he had sold the quarter section. They had encouraged quite a number of relations to come out to Edmonton. A brother and sister lived near and were having a party to which we were all invited – Ronald and I, Henry and the children. It was a good night – just like back home – singing, dancing, drinking and Ian MacFarlane playing the bagpipes. It grew later and later. One by one the children fell asleep. It was four in the morning before we got home. Ronald and Henry lifted the sleeping children and carried them up to bed. And then they were off again – first footing they said – I wasn't one bit pleased about this and let them know it, but they went anyway.

I didn't hear them come back. I was fast asleep.

Later I heard a sad tale of woe – not like Scotland at all – no joy anywhere! They had ended up at a transport cafe at breakfast time where a lone cowboy sat eating apple pie and ice cream – ugg!

Served them right!

Chapter 32

Rescued by the Fire Brigade

Ronald and I found entertainments outside home hard to afford. Not only did they cost a lot but a baby sitter was expensive no matter how young she might be. Canadian children were taught the value of money from the age of two. As soon as they were able to follow older brothers and sisters they would go knocking on doors and asking the occupants for empty bottles which they gave to mothers or fathers to exchange for cents at the supermarket.

We had no television but the programmes I occasionally glimpsed on Carmen's screen did not make me think I was missing much. Most of our entertainment took the form of visiting friends. The friends we visited more than any others were the German couple, Ted Shroers and his wife. They had twin girls of four and a young baby boy born just before we got to know them. On Sundays when we weren't at the lake, they either came to our house or we went to theirs. Ronald got on well with Ted and I with Heidi. We had a lot in common. By coincidence we even ended up with the same doctor. The Shroers lived on the east side of the city near to his surgery. Heidi was having trouble with her four year olds who were still wetting the bed at night. She was impatient with them.

"I just smack zer bottoms until zay are blue and black and still zay wets ze bed," she told me once, adding – "I told the doctor zat and what trouble he makes for me – said I would never stop zem zat way."

There were other customs we heard of, normal to some Germans but anathema to Canadians. The kind of situation that shocked Canadians was couples with young babies going out dancing and leaving their babies tied into cots by tapes attached to sleeping bags – no baby sitter anywhere near. The Germans thought nothing of it. The Canadians were dead against it. It wasn't that the Germans didn't love their children – just a different way of looking at things. I must admit that I thought the latter rather a dangerous custom.

Only once while in Edmonton did Ronald and I go to see a film. Bill Martin, Ronald's boss, tried to encourage us to go to the ten pin bowling ally – a favourite Canadian place of entertainment. We went once or twice but found it too expensive. My main form of outside entertainment was the meetings of the Women's Guild. Something I had found stuffy at home was less so in Canada. A lot of the women members were of the same age as myself. The guild was valuable to me in several ways – in getting to know people, for the entertainments and suppers they occasionally put on and for helping to rid me of an inherent shyness.

"Hold up your head," Ronald had often said to me when going into a crowd of people. "They won't eat you."

As for speaking in public, it was quite beyond me. At some of the Guild functions I learned to do just that as even formal occasions seemed so much less formal and frightening than at home.

On the whole entertainment outside the home was sparse so it was with enthusiasm that I accepted an invitation from Carmen one day. It was just a week or so before my baby was due. It didn't matter. I was desperate to get out – get away from children and constant chores for a short while. The entertainment was rather a strange one but it was free. The way Carmen put it was this.

"You sure don't need to come if you don't want to but I've got two tickets from the mental health board to attend a talk by a fashion model – I guess it's going to make folks feel better to learn how to make the best of themselves. She is also going to give us a few exercises and advice on how to keep slim and fit.

I laughed," She'll have a problem with me at the moment," I said patting my heavily distended stomach.

"Oh you sure won't have to do anything if you don't want to," Carmen said. "It's a scheme thought up by the mental hospital

217

that I was in. They like you to bring a friend along if you can but of course not everyone wants to go to a thing like that – afraid it might be infectious or something. You're very welcome if you want to come. The class is to be held in the Tower Building downtown in the evening. It sure is an impressive place."

A night out for free. I didn't hesitate – it sounded as if it might be fun – different anyway! Carmen got her mother to look after her children and Ronald looked after our lot. Carmen and I set off in the bus. I had a few faltering pains in my stomach but I didn't say anything. I had had similar pains for quite a while before the other children were born. Besides it couldn't be born tonight.

"No baby for a day or two until the Chevy is repaired," Ronald had warned jokingly.

As Carmen had said, the Tower Building was impressive, stretching far up into the darkness – tonight all black glass and concrete. Our meeting room was on the third floor. Fortunately for me there was a lift – saved me from puffing up all these stairs.

The gathering was very odd indeed. The model, Miranda by name, who was to talk to us, was indeed elegant – a beanpole who had wriggled herself into in a knee length dress. Her long fingers nails were red to match the dress – the identical shade – platinum bobbed hair completed the picture with not one hair out of place.

The rest of us were a strange and motley crew of all shapes and sizes. Apart from the model, Carmen was by far the neatest and prettiest there. There were excessively thin women with bulging eyes – squat women – fat women – tall women – tiny women – some that were excitable and some that seemed calm to the point of almost falling asleep. During the talk one or two did actually nod off.

The talk was lively, interesting, helpful and sometimes very entertaining when Miranda had nearly everyone down on the floor doing exercises. She never talked down to us and the women laughed at their own ineptitude as much as they did at each other. Everything was taken in good part – there was a feeling of camaraderie in the air. There was one real comedian among the ladies (up till now I had not met up with many in

Canada) – Rose was her name. Anything less like a rose was hard to imagine. She was dark haired and squat with a plain face and what I can only describe as a Glasgow humour although it was doubtful if she had any Scottish connections. With it she had the happy knack of bringing everyone together.

The evening passed so pleasantly that Miranda had forgotten to look at the elegant gold watch round her elegant slim wrist.

"Holy gee!" she said eventually, "look at the time. It's ten o'clock. We were supposed to be out of here by nine thirty. We'd better get down them stairs quick."

As it was we took the lift. There was no one else about – a deathly silence reigned as we slipped down the floors – the only thing to be heard was the mechanical sound of the lift – for once the women were silent. We went toward the huge doors of darkened glass – they were closed – locked.

Realisation dawned on us all. We were locked in – the only people in the building. Miranda tried various doors on the ground floor – they were all locked. Rose made an outrageous statement. "A bunch of loonies locked in a tower!" she said. Everyone laughed.

Miranda kept cool. "Right folks upstairs again, back to the room we were in. I'll find a phone and we'll be out of here in two tics. Rose, you take over and do some more exercises with the ladies. Carmen, Margaret you come with me and we'll look for a phone." We searched through the rooms on the third floor and finally found an office that was open and had a phone. Miranda eased herself lithely on to the edge of the desk sitting with her elegant legs crossed and dangling. She lifted the receiver – dialled the police station. After a short pause the phone was answered.

"Officer" she said tentatively, "you're not going to believe this but my name is Miranda. I'm a model and I'm locked in the Tower Building with a bunch of women mostly ex-patients from Strathblane Mental Hospital. I've been giving a talk on fashion – didn't notice the time and the caretaker's gone off – locked us in."

There was silence from the other end of the phone for a moment and then I heard rather cynical laughter after which

219

there came the scathing tones of a male voice.

"Oh yeh! I sure have had a of a lot of funny hoaxes in my life but this one takes the cookie – a hostess with a bunch of nuts locked in the tower!"

"Please believe me officer – it's all true. Look, I've got claustrophobics, agoraphobics, manic depressives, schizophrenics, potential suicides, – you name it – they're all here – please believe me and do something – come as quickly as you can. They're OK at the moment but . . .

Just at that moment my stomach which had been acting up all evening in a mild way went into a serious lurch. It must have shown in my eyes because Miranda took her perfect glossy lips away from the phone for a moment.

"You all right?" she said.

"It's the baby. I'm going into labour I think."

"And Officer," Miranda took her hand away from the mouthpiece and spoke into the phone again. "Please do something quickly as one woman has gone into labour."

We waited in the office for the return call. Five minutes felt like an hour – ten minutes an eternity. Miranda and Carmen made me as comfortable as possible in the desk chair. I was feeling fine again only apprehensive. Miranda's long finger nails made a staccato drumming on the desk – at last the phone – the Officer's voice again.

"Sorry for the delay but I've been in touch with the caretaker's wife and she tells me her husband is off to Saskatchewan for the weekend and taken the keys with him." To this day I wonder how he could have been off to Saskatchewan so quickly and why he had taken the keys with him.

"But," continued the Officer, "the fire brigade is on the way – won't be long."

We all trooped to the lift again – there was no panic – all the women behaved calmly. It was Rose who saved the day. For some reason that I will never quite understand, Rose had with her a gold fish bowl of small fish – guppies she called them. Some of the guppies were very fat. Rose was quite convinced that they were pregnant and about to produce. She was quite unaware of my plight and went on about the plight of the fish –

what would happen if they gave birth in the Tower Building. It was all ridiculous in the extreme but Rose had a way of making people laugh at the ridiculous.

Soon the fire engines arrived, their sirens singing loudly in the frosty air, the whirling lights splashing a brilliant orange on the snow-covered sidewalks. The firemen found a bunch of laughing women behind the huge locked glass door. They soon had us out. The chief officer was tall and handsome and enjoying his role as rescuer.

"Hi Clinton," said Carmen in surprised tones. "How are you?"

"Carmen!" he said, "Haven't seen you for the longest time but what the heck are you doing here?"

"Never mind that," she said. "It's a long story but for old time's sake how about a lift home? My friend here is in labour – it would be an act of mercy." She gave a charming irresistible smile. Her lovely Spanish eyes were soft and beguiling.

"Hop in," said the fireman. Easy enough for Carmen – not quite so simple for me but with the strong arms of the chief fire officer to help me, I managed.

"Quick as you can," said Carmen who was enjoying the thrill of it all, as I was also until another contraction hit me. The driver of the fire engine must have noticed my discomfort as he went faster than ever.

"Sure I shouldn't be taking you straight to hospital?" he said.

"No, I'm fine," I said as the contraction passed over. "Going by other births it will be a while yet and I want to tell my husband and get my suitcase."

After that we flew through the night, sirens going, lights flashing, everything in our path making way for us – red lights ignored. This was exciting. I was enjoying it – what a way to have a baby. The noise of the sirens didn't alarm Ronald he told me later. We heard them quite often along our busy thoroughfare. But he did become alarmed when the fire engine stopped outside our door and he saw me being led up the garden path by a fireman. He was at the door to meet us.

"What the . . . ? You all right? The baby?" Ronald who took most things calmly looked deeply concerned.

"Fine," I said. "It's just that it's on its way."

"The Fire Brigade?" Ronald looked completely mystified until he was told the story. The spasm over I was feeling perfectly all right again and invited the firemen and Carmen in for a quick dram.

All we had to offer them was a tot of Ranchmans Special Brew. I believe it is good whisky nowadays but at that time it was the cheapest firewater on the market. Ronald and Henry, once a week, used to purchase half a bottle, time about, from the liquor store and put it in the topmost cupboard in the kitchen – save it for Saturday night. The firemen quickly drained their glasses and disappeared into the night but not before Clinton and Carmen had exchanged addresses. Carmen stayed a little longer to make sure I was all right. What none of them knew was that we had no transport to take us to the hospital.

At that precise moment I saw a car coming from down town direction – a Pontiac – it was Henry. I gave a triumphant yell.

It wasn't long before I was installed in Henry's car with my ready- packed bag in the boot and Ronald at the wheel. Henry's work as a welder had turned out to be quite lucrative and he had been able to afford to buy a car about the same time as we got our new used one. Ronald drove along the empty silent streets.

"Let's have some music," he said. Henry was luckier than us in that he had a radio in his car. Ronald turned the switch and we heard for the first time Andy Stewart singing *The Scottish Soldier*. The song was not long out and had just hit Canada and was to become number one in the charts and played every ten minutes on the radio until even I grew tired of hearing it. But that night in the black interior of Henry's car it hit me like a shot of lightening. It's hard to explain the effect it had on me now that the song has become so well known and, because of that, rather hackneyed. Then it was fresh and the combined Scottish voice, emotion bending music, brave, sad, nostalgic words, spoke directly to me with a kind of glory. I had seen Andy Stewart perform, heard him sing before coming to Canada. His indomitable, perky Scottish personality now stood before me. But it was much more than that. Homesickness swept through me more than it had done since coming to Canada. I saw again

222

the soft contours of the Sidlaw hills, the emerald valley, the silver river and I knew then that however much I grew to love this adopted land I could never think of it as home. Our children might, but for me Scotland would always mean 'hame and destiny'.

> Because these green hills are not high-land hills
> Or the island hills they're not my land's hills
> And fair as these green foreign hills may be
> They are not the hills of home.

"The baby's going to be a boy," Ronald said. "A Scottish soldier."

Chapter 33

Flight over the Rockies

I got home with my new baby after a week in hospital. We had decided before the birth that if it was a boy, we would call him Grant – a Scottish name – a family name and one that Canadians would have difficulty in shortening or pronouncing differently.

Ronald and Henry had scrubbed and cleaned the house so that I would have a happy homecoming. Our children had been staying with the Shroers. Ted's practical wife, Heidi, had offered to take them – wanted nothing for it – said she might call on me some day to do something similar for her. Carmen's three children were being looked after by her landlady Mrs Romanuk. The latter had watched me rather jealously in the past, looking after Carmen's kids and making money that she might have been earning. I wondered if she might want to take over my job altogether. What I did not expect was to get all the children back the day after I arrived home. Mrs Romanuk had had more than enough of them.

Tommy, I expect, was the stumbling block. He was hard to handle for someone who might take him the wrong way.

To begin with, the days after Grant's birth were difficult. By night time I was exhausted but I struggled on and managed to breast feed Grant as I wanted to do. I had done the same for all the others. Fortunately he was a placid baby and slept a lot. Later on, however, he had his times for howling when nothing would pacify him except to carry him upside down under my arm. The rocking motion would put him to sleep. How very handy it would have been to have had one of these backpacks for carrying babies that are commonplace nowadays. I tried unsuccessfully to tie him on my back with a shawl, Gypsy-style, but I hadn't the skill to do it properly and was frightened he would slip out.

Presents began arriving by post for the baby. I hadn't told anyone back home about the expected birth until it happened – not even my mother as I didn't want to worry her. The parcels contained useful clothes for Grant – I didn't need to buy much, what with the presents and what I had left over from Mahri-Louise's baby days.

By Scottish standards the temperatures were very low in that, our third Canadian winter but according to Edmonton standards they were comparatively mild. However, we never felt cold indoors and it was lovely having the sun out almost every day.

Over the winter the sale of acreages etc was poor but we managed to survive. Our finances were in a sorry state once again when just before Easter, Ronald managed to sell an expensive property on the outskirts of Edmonton. He got a good price for it and the commission was substantial.

Mr and Mrs Dacres were the name of the sellers. They were very pleased with the price they got. Mrs Dacres came to know Ronald quite well during the transactions. Knew all about us.

"Why not bring the family out at Easter," said Mrs Dacres. "I would sure like to meet them. Bring them before we move."

And so one afternoon we arrived for tea and cake.

It was a bright day but still winter with a sharpness of frost in the air. The land around us was covered in snow and sparkled brilliantly in the sunshine. I had Grant well wrapped up in a shawl and was standing outside with Ronald and the kids talking to Mr Dacres and admiring the scenery. I wasn't allowed to stand long. The scrawny frame of Mrs Dacres came rushing out from her house, lifted the baby from my arms and rushed back inside with him. When I got in she was sitting nursing him, her kind be-spectacled face watching, worrying in case he had got cold. I thought I would never understand these Canadians.

After Easter a shock awaited us. It came in a phone call from Eileen in Vancouver, Ronald's sister.

"I've just had word from the police." Eileen's worried voice was on the other end of the line. "Father is in a hospital in Los Angeles seriously ill. Harold and I are flying down right away to find out how things are and see what we can do. Seemingly he was on his way to Vancouver. He never told us he was coming.

He'd travelled by ship round Cape Horn. The journey had been a rough one plus he'd forgotten to take his heart pills with him. Never consulted the doctor on board ship. They didn't know about his heart condition until he collapsed. They put him ashore at Los Angeles and into hospital. I'll phone you when I get there – let you know how things are."

We waited anxiously for the next phone call. It came next day. It was Eileen on the line.

"We're back in Vancouver. We've got father home. He'd made a remarkable recovery by the time we got to the hospital at Los Angeles. We were allowed to move him – bring him back here. We managed to get him on a plane. He's still seriously ill. His life still hangs in the balance – can you manage over?"

"I'll arrange it," Ronald said. "Let you know."

The money hadn't come through for the Dacres' acreage yet. Our finances were rock bottom. Without the slightest hesitation Henry said,

"I'll lend you the money to go. I've managed to save a bit since buying the Pontiac."

Henry drove Ronald to the airport at Leduc in time to catch the 1pm flight for Vancouver.

About three in the afternoon the phone rang. I lifted the receiver. It was Ronald I didn't wait for him to speak.

"You've arrived safely – how's things?"

"No I haven't," he said. "I'm back at Leduc airport."

"Back at Leduc airport?" I waited for an explanation.

"Something wrong with the plane. We couldn't make it over the Rockies. The captain told us an engine had conked out. A French girl sitting beside me screamed. She had come from Toronto – 'Not another one?' she said. The air hostess went into hysterics – it was awful but we made it back. They're going to put on another flight – another plane. What do you think I should do?"

Ronald was a brave man – faced most situations calmly – had been through a war – had been on ships when they were sweeping minefields but I knew that the one thing that unnerved him was flying. He must now be very shaken.

"It just couldn't make it over the Rockies," he repeated. "I kept thinking of these jagged peaks."

I had to think fast.

"Oh Ron, I know how it must be for you but I think you should go. You know how you would feel if anything happened to your Dad and you weren't there. The risk of anything being wrong with a different plane is very small. It would be strange indeed if they had trouble with another plane on the same day."

"Thanks, I just needed your reassurance. I'll phone when I get there."

It was three days before Ronald arrived back. He was to be at Leduc airport at first light – would Henry come and collect him? I knew that would be no problem. I very much wanted to be there also so I got Janet, one of Jean Nibyforuk's daughters, to baby sit – stay overnight.

I don't remember much about the run down to Leduc but I do remember vividly, watching the plane taxi-ing to a halt in the half light. When the door of the plane opened and the steel steps were in place, Ronald was one of the first to emerge. He was carrying a huge bunch of flowers. He looked bright and cheerful. Spring had come over the mountains. He was very glad to see us. He handed me the flowers giving me a big hug and shook Henry warmly by the hand thanking him for making his journey possible. He told us that Spring was in Vancouver. It still looked, this frozen morning, as if it would never come here. He also brought with him fresh fish. Apart from those caught in the lake at Nakamun we hadn't tasted fresh fish since coming to Alberta. We were a thousand miles and a vast mountain range from the sea. He told us how good it was to see the sea again.

The news of his father was that of improvement. He was recuperating well at Eileen's. He was coming to see us in a month if things went according to plan.

Chapter 34

Reconciliation

Spring came on us in a rush as it always did in Alberta. The ice rinks melted in the gardens and in the evenings men and women were busy planting seeds that would shoot up at incredible speed. In our area vegetables were of more importance than flowers. In the lakes round Edmonton and all over Alberta, the thick ice was breaking up. I loved to hear the deep booming and the cannonshots of cracking ice which brought winter to an end. The golden orioles were back nesting in the woods and the incredible bluebirds back decorating the air above the prairie.

Father-in-law came – what a joy to see someone from home. I had always got on reasonably well with the 'old man' as Ronald called him. I found him generous and obstinate. The quarrel had always been between father and son. Perhaps, in some ways, they were too alike but now there was a change in the atmosphere. One of mutual respect – the fight was over. Perhaps, in a subtle way, it had been a fight for supremacy but now the 'old man' was facing only a few more years of life.

"Three more years at the most and only if you're careful," Ronald's father had been told when he asked the doctor in Vancouver to tell him the truth.

Whatever it was, the atmosphere was different between the two – the weather had changed. Coming to Canada with a wife and family, coping with all the difficulties, asking no one for help, had been the chief factor in this new respect for son by father. Not even Ronald's bravery during the war had earned it. That was considered to be just doing his duty like his father had done before him. Fortitude in everyday life was what the old man admired – this backbone so revered by Scots.

Before we left Scotland, Ronald's father had vowed he would

never retire from the farm, of which he had the life rent. Now he had come over to tell us he was retiring – wanted to retire. The farm had belonged to Ronald's mother. She had left it to Ronald, her only son, at the end of the day or whenever the father decided to give up. It was Ronald's now. He would have to decide what to do – go back to Scotland and farm three hundred acres of good clay land in the Carse of Gowrie or sell it and return to Canada. His father no longer treated him as a minor – telling him what he must do – the decision was Ronald's alone.

Ronald didn't make up his mind all at once. He was happy with his work here in Canada and he could see it was a land of great opportunity. His father was putting on no pressures. No more being wakened in the middle of the night as he had been as a teenager, to be asked if he was sure he wanted to be a farmer. In order to get peace to go back to sleep Ronald would give the required answer which had to be yes. In Scotland he couldn't discuss things with his father. It had to be father's way or no way. Now it was different

"I'll see," said Ronald. "I'll come back this winter – make up my mind one way or the other. If I do sell up, with the money that I get for the farm, I'd be able to buy so much here. The bargains that I see! Often I think if only I had the money to invest in things myself. Not long ago, Dad, there was a drained lake for sale only twenty miles or so from here. It grows beautiful grass, will make an excellent farm because of that extra bit of moisture it attracts. Empire Real Estate acquired it much to the annoyance of the local farmers who had been using it for years for hay. I got the job of selling it but was warned not to go out to the place alone. 'Take someone with you,' they said in the office, 'another real estate man.' It was sold not long ago to a farmer from Calgary – a real bargain."

While father-in-law was with us another bargain came up – a farm in Drayton Valley – an area that was developing fast. One Saturday we all piled into the car, Ronald's father in the front seat beside his son and me squashed in the back with all the kids. We headed for Drayton Valley.

It was a wonderful day in early summer. Directions took us off the main drag on to what was little more than a track through the bush. The terrain around was hilly and covered in trees – it reminded me of home. Eventually we came to a plain wooden cabin shabby and isolated. There was no one about. The silence was so pronounced you were very much aware of it. The rickety door of the cabin was half open. Ronald pushed it further – went in. There were signs of recent habitation. The fire in the pot-bellied stove wasn't quite out. Everything was in a clutter – no furniture to speak of – a table, chairs, a bunk type bed. We had heard that the owner had always lived there on his own – did a bit of trapping but now he was over seventy and his doctor had said he must live nearer to civilisation.

We had taken a picnic with us. Ronald decided to wait a while to see if he would return. He knew we were coming. The shack was in a hollow surrounded by small hills that swept gently backward. The boys rambled up the grassy slopes and discovered the tiniest of wild strawberries upon which we all feasted. They were very sweet. We followed the track further and came to a babbling river of clearest water not like the muddy Saskatchewan. We had our picnic down by its banks.

Grandpa had enjoyed the easy walk and the feel of wild country. He loved to be with the grandchildren – it made him feel young. We wandered back to the shack after everything was eaten, Ronald carrying Grant, me carrying the picnic basket. Still no human to be seen. We were just about to leave when we heard the thud thud of hooves and a horse appeared through the trees carrying an old man on its back. From either side of the saddle hung bulging saddlebags. He jumped off his horse with amazing agility for a man of over seventy and tied it to a ring on the rock.

"You the real estate guy?" he said to Ronald. "Sure sorry I kept you waiting. I've just been off getting my monthly groceries from the store ten miles away. Didn't think I'd take so darn long."

He insisted we have a cup of coffee – wanted to talk – said he was selling against his better judgement – been in the same place for all his years. This was home; he had known no other. but the doctor had advised him. He might have taken no notice of what he said but everything was going to change anyway – a pipeline was coming through quite near – there would be new roads, nothing would be the same. Also he had not long lost a faithful companion – his dog. It was a bad day, one of the worst in his life, when he had to shoot him but he just wouldn't leave bear cubs alone and thus enraged the mothers. He had nearly lost his life several times over the head of the dog. It was sad that this old timer had to move away. Sometime after father-in-law left, he came to stay with us for a day or two while finalising the sale of his land. He couldn't sleep for the fearful noise – the fridge in our kitchen.

Now that the quarrel was over between Ronald and his father I enjoyed having him with us. He was fond of the children and pampered them. For a time, after he first came, he used to sit on our cheap couch and chuckle. I was curious.

"What amuses you so much?" I asked.

"It's just the contrast," he said, "between Eileen in Vancouver and you here. She lives in the lap of luxury – white carpets, silk bedspreads the latest in electrical equipment etc, beautiful antiques. In fact anything she wants she just has to ask Harold for and she gets it but she grumbles all the time about how awful Canada is. You, on the other hand, in this rickety house with all these kids and very little money, are as happy as sandboys."

One Saturday we took him up to Lake Nakamun with us. It was a sunny day in early summer with the temperature in the seventies. Ronald had given his father a small thermometer – one that Empire Real Estate were giving out as advertising gimmicks. Father-in-law had it in his top pocket. He sat in the shade beside the new cabin that had been built for us at the lake side. He took the thermometer out of his top pocket. Warmed by his body heat it registered 92 degrees. He was most impressed.

"92 in the shade," he said. "That's not bad."

After a month father-in-law left us to fly off to New York to visit a brother he hadn't seen for forty years.

"Are you sure you'll manage on your own?" Ronald said.

"Of course I will, laddie." His tone was firm and so he left us. We had big decisions to make.

Chapter 35

Empire Real Estate, the Greatest!

Henry left us at the beginning of July. He had been with us for almost a year. His work had come to an end in the yard but he had managed to get another job, further south at Blairmore, on the pipeline. We didn't advertise for another lodger as we were uncertain of our movements after the summer months. Besides, Ronald was making a bit more money now and I had more than plenty to do with all the children off school for the summer vacation.

Every weekend we went to Nakamun. The cabin we now had at the lake was a simple but attractive structure made of wood but as yet without furniture of any kind. We missed our white tent in the woods. We had been more comfortable there. Now we slept on sleeping bags on the wooden floor of the cabin which was raised on stilts at the waterside. Sometimes an Arctic wind swept underneath and seeped through the floorboards. However it was safer than the tent in that marauding bears were less likely to break in.

If the nights could be cold, the days were always bright and warm. It was a time of great freedom for the children – a time of sunlight and humming birds, shoals of silver fish, sun-diamonds in the water, the rustle of green leaves, woodsmoke and and the sound of happy men with axes cutting down trees in their lots preparing ground for their cabins. Quite a few more were sold that summer. It was an attractive spot and the lots were not expensive.

The children needed minimum clothes and no shoes. Grant lay a lot in his hammock stretched between two birch trees. I had to keep a watchful eye on Mahri-Louise. Water fascinated her but also made her dizzy. She had to be kept away from the water's edge unless someone was with her.

Weekdays back in Edmonton, when the children were all on holiday, were not quite so bad as I had anticipated. The sunny days found them always outside playing with all the other children. There was a great sense of freedom for children in Canadian towns. They went barefoot by choice, loving to feel the hot sidewalks under their active feet. For a couple of weeks Ronnie, now four years old, went to a summer school. He had made friends with the three little girls next door who were looked after by their grandparents. They were a Pentecostal family and their church was running a summer school for children. The Foxes had asked me if they could take Ronnie along with them.

"The girls sure want him to go with them," Mrs Fox said to me one day.

Ronnie liked the idea. He was dying to go to something called school like the big boys. We got him a school satchel which made him feel on top of the world and off he would go every morning with Mrs Fox and the girls, his red hair gleaming in the early sunlight. He wasn't shy and enjoyed the summer school immensely. This dramatic religion suited his dramatic temperament. Religion wasn't out of fashion in Edmonton but many people didn't worry about which

At the end of the month Empire Real Estate held a steak and beans dinner for its salesmen. Top salesman and wife got steak – the others got beans.

church they went to. Many had no great allegiance to any church. Carmen, a Catholic, didn't mind at all when her boys were determined to go to the Presbyterian Church with our boys. Rupert Street Presbyterian Church was close by and had a good Sunday school. Children of several denominations went because it was close and accessible with a pleasant young minister in charge.

In August Ronald was top salesman of the month for the second time running. Always at the end of the month Empire Real Estate held a steak and beans dinner for its salesmen. Top salesman and wife got steak – the others got beans. Ronald had always refused to take me to these do's. He could see through Empire Real Estate tricks – get the wives into competition for the steak. Not that it was the steak they cared about but the honour of their husband being the top salesman. The theory behind it was that the women would harangue the men to work harder. Ronald would not go along with that way of working.

"I may have to be humiliated into eating beans, but I am not having my wife treated that way," was the stance Ronald took. "I am employed by Empire Real Estate – my wife is not," he told them and so I never went.

The steak and beans dinner was held at the end of August. When he came home from the event Ronald told me of all the razamataz.

"Worse than usual," he said. "One of the head bummers stood up and said what a marvellous firm Empire Real Estate is – greatest in Alberta if not the whole of Canada – how well it had done over the last few years with its wonderful salesmen of which, I tonight, was the shining example. He told us what an honour it was to work for such a firm."

I laughed. Sitting beside him on our cheap couch I put my arm round his waist and gave him a hug. "Just the same I'm proud of you Ron. No one can say you haven't worked for that firm."

Next day when Ronald came home at tea time I could see something was the matter even before he spoke. He had a stunned expression on his face.

"I just don't believe it," he said. "After last night – after all that was said – I just don't believe it!"

I waited for an explanation.

"Empire Real Estate is closing down at the end of next month, going out of business. No explanation – nothing. We were all told we would have to find other jobs. After what was said last night it seems incredible."

It was like a bolt from the blue. At first I was too stunned to say anything and then, "That's Canada for you," I said. "A volatile society – always moving on."

In a way, for us, it was a good thing – made it easier for Ronald to come to a definite decision. He had made enough money during the summer for us all to fly home. He had to go home anyway and he had no intention of leaving me and the children behind. He could make definite arrangements now. We would go in September.

Next day Carmen paid me a visit. She had special news. I could see she was happy and excited. Before I could get a word in she had blurted it all out.

"I'm getting married to Clinton in October and then we're going to America to live." I was so happy for her I gave her a big hug.

"How lovely," I said. "I thought there was something in the wind."

"But how about you folks?" she said looking anxious.

"We're leaving," I said. "Just knew yesterday for sure. Ronald has to go home to settle up his affairs and we're going with him. Empire Real Estate is closing down but we may be back."

"Somehow I don't think you will," said Carmen. "You've had a tough time here and from what you've told me you've a lot to go back to. Many immigrants do go back home and quite a few return. But the ones that come back have little to go home for. That doesn't seem to be the case with you. Anyhow I wish you the best of luck and thank you for making it possible for me to get on my feet again."

And so this volatile society was moving on – others in the street were going also – nothing or nobody stayed still for long. This strange mixture of people had shared for a while the same environment, similar troubles, happinesses, sorrows to disperse tomorrow – mostly never to meet again.

reddest apples I had ever seen. We stopped the car to buy some and were served by an enormously fat man in a red shirt with a round stomach that resembled nothing so much as a very much exaggerated Mackintosh Red.

Gradually we made our way over the Cascade mountains – older and gentler than the Rockies and very beautiful. We lingered on this wonderful high terrain with its clear rivers and bright colours of autumn – not unlike the Highland mountains back home. We stayed the night in a log-cabin-cum-motel that smelt deliciously of pinewood smoke. And then next day we travelled on through Seattle and on to Vancouver that most impressive city on the shores of the Pacific with its backdrop of magnificent mountains.

Thoroughly spoiled by Eileen and Harold in a house with white angora carpets, silken quilts and antique furniture, we stayed two weeks in Vancouver. At the front of their split level house there was a balcony to walk out on facing Vancouver's magnificent bridge – a long balcony bright with exotic plants and where Japanese mobiles, made from fragile panels of glass, fluttered in the breeze with a mysterious eastern tinkle.

Although I was very much enjoying our stay with Eileen and Harold – the opulence, the beautiful scenery, the freedom from worry and the comparative rest, I was eager to get home. Now that the event was so close I couldn't wait to see my mother and father again. They had been a great support to us, always sending useful parcels and writing helpful, cheerful letters. They never complained that they were missing out on seeing us or their only grandchildren growing so quickly. Always optimistic, they never let us feel downhearted. I was dying to let them see our new babies and have them wonder at how their grandchildren had grown. No one on earth would be more interested.

I was also longing to see my country again in all its moods and weathers – its soft greyness, its storms, its idyllic days more appreciated because they were less frequent.

I did not know whether we would come back to this land that I had learned to love. I knew now that I could be happy in either country. I also knew that if we did come back, the pull of the place where I was born and raised would always be strong.

I was going back home a different person. Canada had taught me a great deal about myself and what were really the most important things in life. It had taught me that most things can be done without, provided there is enough food, water and heat. Many things I might have thought of as essential at home weren't really, even tables and chairs.

I had learned a lot about humanity. We had met people of many nationalities and discovered, as I had always suspected, that the likenesses were stronger than the differences. That in each race there were the generous and the kind, the mean and the greedy.

I had learned the pleasure of the camaraderie that can rise up between people when they come face to face with similar difficulties and how very kind complete strangers can be for no reason. One wise saying I knew I would never forget. It was told to me by Eunice, the neighbour in Edmonton who taught me how to bake bread. Her mother, an early pioneer, talking about her own difficult life in Alberta had once said,

"I have had a lot of help from people during my lifetime and likewise I have helped many people. Not always the same people, but I guess it works out about even."

I was going back to Scotland a much more confident person – one who would find it less difficult to hold her head up and speak in public – one who would be able to cope with most situations. Going back also with much more appreciation of the British way of life and the Scottish in particular. It was perhaps we who had been in the doldrums not the country. But not any more – after Canada anything seemed possible. I would, however, appreciate the feeling of safety I had always felt at home which we never quite felt in Canada with its nine months winter when so much had to close down because of the severity of the climate. Could there ever be work for everyone in the winter in this huge frozen country?

Most of all, perhaps, I looked forward to going back to a solid family farmhouse with its rowan tree in the garden to ward off trouble and bring good luck.